W9-AGK-919

The World Book of Word Power

THE

WORLD BOOK OF

WORD POWER

Volume 1

Language

World Book, Inc.
a Scott Fetzer company
Chicago   London   Sydney   Toronto

Staff

Project management and design
Acacia Creative Services
Judi Biss, project director
Luis Ramirez, creative director

Project editor
Joan A. Grygel

Chapter editors
India Cooper
Judith Gallagher
Mary Oates Johnson
Joyce Senn

The World Book of Word Power is based on these previous
World Book publications: *World Book Complete Word Power
Library; Winning with Words; Grammar and Style Guide* from
the *World Book Desk Reference Set.*

© 1991 World Book, Inc. All rights reserved. This volume
may not be reproduced in whole or in part in any form
without prior written permission from the publisher.

World Book, Inc.
525 West Monroe
Chicago, IL 60606

Printed in the United States of America

ISBN 0-7166-3238-1
Library of Congress Catalog Card
No. 90-72119
A/IA

Cover Photo
E. Wells, *A New Map of the Terraqueous Globe*
Printed in Oxford, England, circa 1701
Courtesy of George Ritzlin Books & Maps

Acknowledgments

Page 409: The story of the Christian and the lion is reprinted from
HOW TO BE THE LIFE OF THE PODIUM ©1982 by S. H.
Simmons by permission of Sylvia Simmons.

Page 412: "The Let-Down" is from THE PUBLIC SPEAKER'S
TREASURE CHEST, Third Edition, by Herbert V. Prochnow
and Herbert V. Prochnow, Jr. Copyright 1942 by Harper &
Row Publishers, Inc. Copyright ©1964, 1977 by Herbert V.
Prochnow and Herbert V. Prochnow, Jr. Reprinted by
permission of HarperCollins Publishers.

Page 428: The two speech openers are from the book SPEAKERS ON
THE SPOT by Edgar Bernhard ©1977. Used by permission
of the publisher, Park Publishing/A division of Simon &
Schuster, West Nyack, NY.

Page 443: Excerpt from "I Have a Dream" reprinted by permission of
Joan Daves. Copyright ©1963 by Martin Luther King, Jr.

Page 445: "Silence" reprinted with permission of Macmillan Publishing
Company from COLLECTED POEMS by Marianne Moore.
Copyright 1935 by Marianne Moore, renewed 1963 by
Marianne Moore and T. S. Eliot.

Page 446: Excerpt from "The Road Not Taken" is from THE POETRY
OF ROBERT FROST edited by Edward Connery Lathem.
Copyright 1916, ©1969 by Holt, Rinehart and Winston.
Copyright 1944 by Robert Frost. Reprinted by permission of
Henry Holt and Company, Inc.
"Dream Boogie," from MONTAGE OF A DREAM DEFERRED,
by Langston Hughes, is reprinted by permission of Harold
Ober Associates Incorporated. Copyright 1951 by Langston
Hughes. Copyright renewed 1979 by George Houston Bass.

Page 459: *Valedictory Speech* reprinted by permission of Lynn Marie
Bowen-Mafera, Mary A. Campbell, Jennifer Gill, Joanne
Hubbard, Jill Hubbard-Meinzer, and Erin C. Miller.

Page 472: Excerpts from the *Northwestern Endicott Report 1975*, by
Frank S. Endicott, copyright 1975 by Northwestern
University. Reprinted by permission of Victor R. Lindquist.

Page 473: Excerpts from the *Northwestern Lindquist-Endicott Report
1983*, by Victor R. Lindquist, copyright 1982 by Northwestern
University. Reprinted by permission of Victor R. Lindquist.

Page 484: Excerpt from "How to Clear Lines of Communication," by
Dr. Edgar Dale and Dr. Jeanne Chall, by permission of
Dr. Jeanne Chall. Published in EDUCATIONAL TRENDS,
January 1950, by Croft Educational Services.

Page 503: Questions for parent/teacher conferences excerpted from
YOU CAN IMPROVE YOUR CHILD'S SCHOOL by William
Rioux, copyright ©1980 by National Committee for Citizens
in Education. Reprinted by permission of William Rioux.

Contents

Introduction

The Purpose of *The World Book of Word Power*

Probably the single most important task facing every one of us on a daily basis is effective communication. Of course, the primary method of communication between people is words. Words are the collections of sounds and symbols we have assigned to describe our experiences, emotions, and ideas. Words are abstract labels that may be arranged and rearranged to communicate a variety of meanings in a variety of ways—either written or spoken.

The World Book of Word Power has been developed specifically to help you increase your overall ability to use words—in your everyday personal life, at school, in business situations, and when participating in civic activities. "Word power," the collection of skills and techniques that enable a person to communicate effectively, is perhaps the most vital area for personal growth that you will ever encounter. Success in school, effectiveness on the job, enjoyment of social interaction, and warmth in personal relationships—all depend greatly on the extent of your ability to use your word power.

How to Use This Book

The World Book of Word Power is a reference handbook for home and office use designed for quick look-up of answers to questions about written and spoken language. Use of italics in the text is your signal that a straightforward definition is being provided. For example, "An *adjective* is a word that modifies a noun or a pronoun." In addition, there are numerous models, descriptions, and examples that can be readily adapted for your specific needs—all without having to wade through lengthy explanations.

Examples are set apart from the text on separate lines in this distinctive type style.

Cross-References. Perhaps most important of all, you can easily locate related information through the cross-references that are provided right when you need them. The entire numbering system, combined with "guide word" headings at the top of each right-hand page, helps you rapidly locate the information you seek. The first number in the cross-referencing system is the chapter number. Capital letters, used in alphabetical order within each chapter, set off major sections. As in basic outline form, subsections are numbered, and sub-subsections have lower case letters in alphabetical order. For example, "*see* **4.A.2.e**: Interrogative Pronouns" directs you to Chapter 4 ("Grammar"), section A ("Parts of Speech"), subsection 2 ("Pronouns"), sub-subsection e ("Interrogative Pronouns"). Because the cross-reference includes the title of the related item, you can decide immediately whether or not you need to turn to that section for additional information on your specific question.

Notes. Two kinds of notes direct your attention to important aspects not to be overlooked. Book notes, marked by the symbol shown in the outside margin, provide tips on the interrelationship of information across chapters. Such notes help you use the book more effectively by pointing out where critical background information can be found that is a foundation for the topics discussed within the present chapter.

Chapter notes are represented by the symbol shown in the outside margin. These notes point out exceptions to the guidelines being discussed or emphasize implications for practical application of the discussion.

Special Features. Throughout the book you will find additional information set off in colored boxes within the text. These special features present ancillary information that may be of interest, such as extended excerpts, exercises, how-to information, tables and charts, and historical background information.

Book Organization

The two volumes of *The World Book of Word Power* are "Language" and "Writing and Speaking." The first volume, Part I, includes the basic principles of language presented in an easy-to-understand way. Part I is designed to provide you with a thorough foundation in the rules that promote "word power."

The second volume helps you apply the guidelines for effective communication described in Part I to both written (Part II) and spoken (Part III) communication. You can immediately apply the abundant tips, examples, and advice found in "Writing and Speaking" to practical writing or speaking situations.

The following brief synopsis of each chapter will help you get an overview of the rich, varied content at your fingertips.

Part I: Language. Chapter 1, The English Language, includes a brief history of the English language and an overview of some of its vibrant and energetic ongoing changes. A basic understanding of and appreciation for the history and continuing evolution of the language can help you assimilate the information in the remaining chapters in Part I.

In Chapter 2, Word Structure and Vocabulary, you will learn how to build your vocabulary by analyzing word structure such as word roots and affixes. Other approaches to vocabulary building that are presented include recognizing synonym and antonym relationships, using context as clues to word meaning, understanding the denotation and connotation of words, and interpreting figures of speech. In addition, you will find out how a dictionary can help you unlock the meanings of many unfamiliar words. The chapter also includes a list of specialized words to help you enrich your vocabulary base.

Chapter 3, Spelling, presents guidelines for improving spelling. By following such guidelines, becoming aware of common mispronunciations, and knowing which letters or group of letters spell the same sound in English, you can become a more effective speller. Learning spelling rules that apply to a large percentage of English words, knowing the difference between spellings of homophones, as well as mastering frequently misspelled words also can improve your spelling ability.

Using proper grammar is an essential part of communicating clearly and effectively. In Chapter 4,

Grammar, you will learn how to identify the eight parts of speech, the parts of a sentence, and the different kinds of sentences.

It's important to choose the right words and use them correctly if you want to convey your meaning clearly to your audience. Chapter 5, Usage and Style, discusses correct word use in both formal and informal situations. It includes commonly misused constructions and proper forms of address.

Chapter 6, Mechanics, includes rules for capitalization and punctuation. Mastering these rules can impart clarity to your writing.

Part II: Writing. Chapter 7, The Writing Process, reviews planning, drafting, revising, and editing. The chapter provides guidelines for developing any piece of nonfiction writing and is a basis for developing specific kinds of writing discussed in the other chapters in Part II.

The first half of Chapter 8, Kinds of Writing, covers the four basic kinds of writing: expository, descriptive, narrative, and argumentative. The second half of the chapter presents another way of understanding writing—by dividing it into nonfiction, fiction, and poetry. Each section discusses the major elements and reviews the various forms of each type of writing.

Chapter 9, Personal Writing, presents guidelines and models for those occasions when only letters are suitable: thank-you letters, letters of congratulation and condolence, and apologies. The chapter also presents models and guides for formal and informal invitations, replies, and announcements.

Success in school probably depends more on your ability to express yourself clearly and correctly in writing than on any other ability or skill. Chapter 10, School Writing, reviews the basic procedures for the most common types of writing required in school, including short reports, book reports, term papers, and essay questions.

Chapter 11, Manuscript Preparation and Editing, helps you correctly present your term paper for school or your material for publication. The steps in preparing a manuscript include formatting, revising, and arranging; proofreading; and preparing footnotes and a bibliography. A separate section deals with the special considerations that apply if you are going to generate manuscript by computer.

Clear, concise writing is one of the most important tools of business. Chapter 12, Business Writing, presents instructions for preparing some of the basic forms of business communication: résumés and cover letters, business letters of various types, reports, proposals, memorandums, want ads, and facsimile transmittals.

Chapter 13, Civic Writing, consists of models and guidelines for writing letters to the editor or to elected officials, news releases, television or radio announcements, and newsletters concerning events and issues of importance to society.

Part III: Speaking. Whether you are interviewing for a job, giving a formal speech, expressing your opinion at a town meeting, or calling a dealership to price a new car, being an effective speaker will help you accomplish your purpose. Chapter 14, the Spoken Word, is a foundation for all other chapters in Part III. It provides you with the basic knowledge you need to speak clearly, pleasantly, and effectively in any speaking situation. In this chapter, you will learn how to control your voice, your body, and other speaking tools and how to stay in control while you are speaking. The chapter also presents the fundamentals for preparing and developing a speech and for the other half of verbal communication—listening.

The telephone has become indispensable for most of us. It quickly puts people in touch with their families and friends and is a powerful business tool. Furthermore, there is no substitute for a telephone in an emergency. Chapter 15, Telephoning, is about how to use it effectively in personal, business, and emergency situations.

Chapter 16, Speaking at School, helps you participate effectively in the classroom when asking or answering questions, giving book reports and other kinds of oral reports, and contributing to group discussions. You will learn about debates, orations, and other formal speaking occasions. You will also learn how meetings are conducted according to the rules of parliamentary procedure.

Every job requires that you speak to a co-worker, a boss, or a subordinate. Speaking is your strongest vehicle for communicating in the business world. Chapter 17, Speaking at Work, helps you speak effectively and with confidence in employment interviews, performance appraisals, interviews to handle on-the-job problems, and business meetings. You will learn how to give an effective business report and how to speak to customers when selling. Finally, you will learn how to make the most of speaking opportunities in informal business situations such as business meals and conventions.

Your daily life in the community is filled with speaking occasions. For most of these occasions you will have—and need—no specific preparation. Still, knowing how to communicate effectively is important. In Chapter 18, Speaking in the Community, you will learn strategies for communicating at meetings and social events, in commercial and professional transactions, and with family and friends.

Since many topics presented in this book are treated in greater detail elsewhere, an appendix lists other helpful resources to answer your communication questions. Finally, a detailed index helps you readily locate the information you seek for your own word-power question.

Language

The English Language

The English language has grown from a variety of roots over the ages. Even today it continues to grow and change. Following is a brief history of the English language and an overview of some of its vibrant and energetic ongoing changes.

A basic understanding of and appreciation for the history and continuing evolution of the language can help you assimilate the information in the remaining chapters in this section.

1.A — The History of English

The history of the English language is usually divided into three major periods: Old English (or Anglo-Saxon); Middle English; and Modern English.

1.A.1 — Old English

Until about A.D. 450, England was not called England, nor was English spoken there. Before that time, the country was called Britain and the people were known as Britons. The Britons spoke Celtic dialects, which included many Latin words because Roman troops occupied Britain from A.D. 43 until the mid-400's.

Around 450, invading Germanic tribes called Angles, Saxons, Jutes, and Frisians conquered Britain. These conquerors all spoke similar dialects of Germanic. The Angles and Saxons occupied a large part of Britain, which took its new name, *England,* from the name of the Angles. From the 500's to 1066, the Anglo-Saxon language, now usually called Old English, became firmly established.

Celtic made only a small contribution to the Old English vocabulary. Except for a few words such as *crag* and *bin*, most Celtic words that remain in English today are place names such as *Avon, Kent, London*, and *Thames*.

Latin had a much stronger influence on early English. Even before the Germanic tribes invaded Britain, the Britons had borrowed many words, such as *camp* and *wine*, from their Latin-speaking rulers. During the 500's, Latin-speaking Celt and Roman missionaries spread Christianity in England, and more Latin words entered the English vocabulary at that time. Most of these words were religious terms such as *bishop* and *mass*.

In the 800's, Vikings from Denmark and Norway invaded England and many of these Scandinavians settled in England and intermarried with the English. Many English words have their origin in the Scandinavian languages, among them most words that begin with *sk* (for example, *sky, skill*, and *skirt*). Especially important were the Scandinavian pronouns that replaced English pronouns. *They, them*, and *their* took the place of words that today would probably have been something like *hie, hem*, and *her*.

The following sentence from a document written in 1020 shows what Old English looked like. (The letter þ, called *thorn*, represents the sound spelled *th*.)

Ic nam me to gemynde þa gewritu and þa word þe se arcebiscop Lyfing me fram þam papan brohte of Rome.
(I have remembered the writs and the words that Archbishop Lyfing brought me from the Pope of Rome.)

Notice that some words in the example are exactly the same as words still used today. Some are slightly different but still recognizable. Notice, too, the arrangement of the words in the example. Translated word for word, the last part would say ". . . that Archbishop Lyfing me from the Pope brought of Rome."

1.A.2
Middle English

In 1066, the Normans invaded Britain, replacing the English people as the chief landholders and church officials. The invaders' language—the Norman dialect of French—became the language of the ruling class. The common people, however, continued to speak English.

Norman-French and English existed side by side until political and social changes began to favor the use of English by all classes. By the end of the Middle English period (1100–1500), English had again established itself as the major language in Britain. But, as a result of the Norman Conquest, thousands of French words had entered the English vocabulary—words such as *air, army, art, blue, chair, color, dinner, government, jolly, judge, justice, mayor, paper, poet, prison,* and *towel.* Words from other languages also became part of English during this period, including words of Dutch origin such as *deck, easel, etch, freight, furlough,* and *stoop.*

The Norman Conquest accelerated changes that had already begun to occur in English grammar and pronunciation patterns. Special word endings, called *inflections,* lost their distinctive meanings, and word order instead of word endings became the key to the meaning of a sentence.

The Modern English adjective *happy* can be compared in two ways: by inflection and by word order. An *inflection* is a variation in the form of a word to show case, number, gender, person, tense, mood, voice, or comparison.

I am happy.	The adjective *happy* is in the positive form.
I am happier.	The adjective *happy* is in the comparative form.
I am the *happiest.*	The adjective *happy* is in the superlative form.

The ending *-y,* the ending *-er,* and the ending *-est* all show meaning. The same meanings can also be conveyed by adding words in a certain order; that is, by using words instead of inflections:

I am happy.	The adjective *happy,* with no accompanying word, is in the positive form.
I am more happy.	The adjective *happy,* preceded by the word *more,* is in the comparative form.
I am the most happy.	The adjective *happy,* preceded by the word *most,* is in the superlative form.

The following sentence is an example of Middle English. It comes from a proclamation made by King Henry in 1258. (The letter that looks like a *3* is called *yogh*. It was used as the sound *gh* at the end of a word.)

Henri bur3 Godes fultume King on Engleneloande Lhoauerd on Yrloande Duk on Normandi on Aquitaine and Eorl on Aniow send igretinge to alle hise holde.
(Henry, by the grace of God [through God's help], King of England, Lord of Ireland, Duke of Normandy and Aquitaine, and Earl of Anjou, sends greetings to all his subjects.)

1.A.3 Modern English

The Modern English period, starting about 1500, witnessed the standardization of the language. Several factors contributed to establishing standard English spelling and certain forms of usage. Among these factors are the introduction of the printing press into England in 1477, the revival of interest in literature, and the growth of popular education. Since printing allowed books to be created in much greater numbers than handwritten books of previous centuries ever could have been, the spelling and usage within those printed books gained a greater acceptance. The revival of interest in literature, especially in classical Greek and Latin literature, led to attempts to label grammar and some spelling as "right" or "wrong." The coincidental growth of popular education enabled this standardization brought to English through printing and the literary revival to be quickly spread.

From the 1500's through the 1700's, more than 10,000 new words entered the language. Many of these were taken from Latin and Greek by scholars who wanted to replace words earlier adopted from French. More than 25 percent of modern English words come almost directly from classical languages. These words include *conduct, dexterity, extinguish, scientific,* and *spurious.*

Because of these and other borrowings (including borrowings from French, Italian, Spanish, Russian, German, American Indian, and Arabic), English today has a larger and more varied vocabulary than almost any other language. The following lists show sources of some words that are now firmly entrenched in English-speakers' vocabularies. *See also* **Chapter 2**: Word Structure and Vocabulary.

Sources of Some English Words

LATIN	GREEK	FRENCH	GERMAN
anchor	apostle	captain	cobalt
butter	chlorine	castle	dachshund
chalk	church	fry	delicatessen
circle	comet	horrible	hamster
data	demon	juggler	nickel
education	idiosyncrasy	jury	noodle
equal	oligarchy	magic	plunder
janitor	paper	prince	poodle
kitchen	pathos	question	pretzel
library	phone	royal	quartz
medium	telegram	secret	waltz
orbit	xylophone	soldier	yodel

DUTCH	ITALIAN	SPANISH	SCANDINAVIAN
buoy	balcony	alligator	fellow
coleslaw	balloon	barbecue	kick
cruise	broccoli	canyon	law
duffel	carnival	chocolate	rag
easel	duet	guitar	rug
frolic	ghetto	mosquito	saga
landscape	opera	patio	score
luck	solo	rodeo	scowl
pickle	trombone	tango	ski
spool	umbrella	tomato	skin
wagon	violin	tornado	skirt
yacht	volcano	vanilla	window

ARABIC	CELTIC	INDIAN	ORIENTAL
algebra	bog	bandanna	chow
almanac	brogue	bungalow	geisha
candy	clan	cot	judo
cotton	crag	curry	ju-jitsu
giraffe	galore	jungle	ketchup
hazard	leprechaun	loot	kimono
magazine	plaid	pajamas	silk
mattress	shamrock	shampoo	soy
sugar	slogan	thug	tea
syrup	tory	yoga	tycoon

PACIFIC ISLANDS	SLAVIC	AFRICAN	SEMITIC
bamboo	coach	banjo	amen
boomerang	czar	gorilla	cherub
gingham	goulash	gumbo	hallelujah
kangaroo	mammoth	jazz	jubilee
luau	paprika	rumba	kosher
parakeet	polka	samba	matzo
rattan	soviet	tote	rabbi
taboo	steppe	voodoo	
tattoo	tundra	yam	
ukulele			

Editor's note: Some of these words, though ultimately from the given language, entered English via other languages. Also, many English words have come from other languages not mentioned here, such as North and South American Indian languages, Portuguese, Persian, and Turkish.

1.B
Continuing Evolution of the English Language

The English language has evolved over time into the form we read, write, hear, and speak today. This expansion and change is constantly proceeding.

Look at any new edition of a dictionary. Compared to its previous edition, it includes new words; new definitions for previously existing words; variations in spellings, and perhaps in pronunciations; and changes in word usage notes. The updated dictionary may drop some words that have faded from use to make room for the new entries. Such changes are made only after considerable study of prevalent usage.

1.B.1
Vocabulary Growth

As inventions are created, new discoveries made, and additional words are borrowed or "coined," the English language continues to grow. *See also* **2.H**: Words Worth Knowing.

Some English terms that were not in use twenty years ago include: *modem, AIDS, star wars, Medicare, compact disc,* and *yuppie.*

1.B.2
Spelling Changes

The present English alphabet and its corresponding sounds have been standardized for more than a century. However, the accepted spelling of relatively new terms may change over time.

For example, with frequent use, many two-word combinations come to be recognized as compound words. These compounds eventually may become hyphenated terms or even closed up as one word.

Data base may be spelled only as *database* with increased usage.

Likewise, from variant spellings of new terms, a generally accepted spelling emerges.

Disc jockey may eventually be spelled only as *disk jockey* or vice versa.

In a similar vein, acronyms (the initial letters of a group of words) become recognized as individual words that can stand alone.

WYSIWYG (pronounced "wizzy-wig"), an acronym for "what you see is what you get" on a computer monitor, may become a standard word as has *scuba,* an acronym for "self-contained underwater breathing apparatus"

Such developments occur gradually. Therefore, a thorough understanding of spelling rules and guidelines (*see* **Chapter 3**: Spelling), together with an up-to-date dictionary are useful tools for all writers.

1.B.3 Grammar and Usage Evolution

Throughout the ages, people have attempted to codify the English language in order to explain its basic operating principles of use. *Grammar* is a set of principles by which a language functions. All English grammar and usage "rules" are really guidelines to help ensure clear communication. *See* **Chapter 4**: Grammar *and* **Chapter 5**: Usage and Style.

Grammar and usage guidelines do not remain completely unchanged from age to age. Just as we may look back at a line from Chaucer or Shakespeare and find the language quaint or old-fashioned, future generations will surely find "oddities" in the language we use today.

As the language evolves, so do the approaches to grammar. Following are brief explanations of three approaches to the study of the English language. Notice how each grammar system gives a different perspective on how English functions. Although structural and transformational grammar are rarely applied today in their pure forms, these explanations complement one another, highlighting different aspects of the language and strengthening the overall understanding of English. Many teachers of English grammar use ideas from several grammar descriptions to help their students understand how English functions.

1.B.3.a
Traditional Grammar

Traditional grammar treats the parts of speech as the building blocks for every sentence. Words are labeled as belonging to one of the eight parts of speech: *nouns, verbs, pronouns, adjectives, adverbs, prepositions, conjunctions,* and *interjections.* The word's part of speech depends upon its formal features and its function or position in a sentence.

> Both *table* and *man* are nouns because they show the formal features of the possessive form (*table's, man's*) and the plural form (*tables, men*). Both *table* and *man* can also fill a position or function in a sentence, such as "The _____ is big."

Nouns, verbs, adjectives, and adverbs can be defined by formal features and function or position. Other parts of speech, such as prepositions and conjunctions, have no formal features. They can be identified by their function or position in a sentence.

Many words can be classified as more than one part of speech, depending on how they are used.

> The room was decorated in *yellow.* (noun)
> The *yellow* dress needed pressing. (adjective)
> Dry cleaning will *yellow* that fabric. (verb)

1.B.3.b
Structural Grammar

Structural grammar describes how sounds, word forms, and word positions affect meaning. Structural grammar concerns itself with two meanings in each sentence, the lexical meaning and the structural meaning. The *lexical meaning* is the dictionary meaning of the words. The *structural meaning* comes from how the words are formed and where they are positioned in the sentence. To illustrate the difference, look at the following example.

> *The groby stils kraded mitly.*

Except for *The,* this sentence is made up of words with no dictionary meaning. Yet it still reads like a sentence and, according to structural grammar, it has a structural meaning. That is, the words follow a familiar pattern that indicates "more than one thing acted in some manner."

According to structural linguistics, the word *stils* is recognized as a noun because it has a plural ending, *-s,* and is marked by the article *the.*

Groby is an adjective because it appears between an article and a noun and has a typical adjective ending, *-y.*

Kraded is recognized as a verb because it has a position in the sentence that is typical for verbs, and because *-ed* is a common past tense verb ending.

Mitly is an adverb because it ends in *-ly,* a typical adverb ending, and because it appears in a typical adverb position in the sentence.

Note that the structural meaning emerges from word order and word endings. The "sentence" can be given lexical meaning by substituting dictionary words:

The weary cows walked slowly.

In structural grammar, words such as *weary* (adjective), *cows* (noun), *walked* (verb), and *slowly* (adverb) are called "content" or "form class" words. "Function words" such as *the, might, can, rather, very,* and *somewhat* are used to connect form class words to one another and to show how they relate to one another in a sentence.

1.B.3.c Transformational Grammar

Transformational grammar attempts to explain how people are able to produce all of the possible sentences of a language—even sentences they may never have heard or read before.

In transformational grammar, all sentences are divided into basic, or kernel, sentences, and sentences that are transformations. A *kernel sentence* is a simple declarative sentence. *Transformations* are the result of adding, deleting, or rearranging the words of a kernel sentence.

Kernel sentence:
The cans are full.

Transformation to a negative sentence:
The cans are not full. (add *not*)

Transformation to an imperative sentence:
Fill the cans. (delete words)

Transformation to an interrogative sentence:
Are the cans full? (rearrange)

Any complicated sentence can be traced to kernel sentences.

The tall man who arrived late spoke out.

Kernel sentences:
The man spoke out. The man was tall. The man arrived. The man was late.

1.B.3.d
Grammar Today

The underlying premises of the three previously described systems have been melded into our current approach to the study of grammar. In addition, the grammar of today includes flexibility when applying the basic guidelines. Today we recognize that the "correctness" of grammar and usage varies according to the context in which it is spoken or written. Constructions that are appropriate in one setting could be inappropriate in another and vice versa. Some important considerations involved in "bending the rules" (*see* **5.C**: Bending the Rules) include:

- who will be reading or hearing what you have to communicate
- whether the situation is formal or informal
- the purpose of the communication.

The English language is dynamic and ever-changing. But the formal grammar of standard English changes far less frequently. The grammar guidelines of today will still be acceptable in years to come.

Word Structure and Vocabulary

Building your vocabulary involves analyzing *word structure,* or the elements that make up many words. These elements include word roots and affixes. Other approaches to vocabulary building include recognizing synonym and antonym relationships, using context as clues to word meaning, understanding the denotation and connotation of words, and interpreting figures of speech. In addition, by using a dictionary you can unlock many unfamiliar words. You can also enrich your vocabulary base by determining which words you know from a list of specialized words.

A *root* is a word or a word part from which other words can be made. The roots of many English words come from Greek and Latin. Words that are members of the same family of meaning often are formed from the same root.

2.A

Roots

Many words dealing with believing and trusting are formed from the Latin root *cred* (believe, trust): *credit, credibility, incredible, incredulous.*

Knowledge of roots can help you determine the meaning of unfamiliar words.

If you know that the Latin roots *scrib* and *script* have to do with writing, you will have important clues to the meaning of words such as *scribble, scribe, transcribe, describe, manu-script, prescription,* and *scripture.*

The following is a list of some of the most important roots used in English words.

ROOT	MEANING	SAMPLE WORDS
acro	height, high, tip, end	acrophobia, acrobat, acronym, acropolis
agr	field, land	agriculture, agrarian, agronomy, peregrinator
alg, algos	pain	nostalgia, analgesic, neuralgia, cardialgia
ali	another	alias, alien, unalienable, alienate
alt	tall, high	altitude, alto, altimeter, exalt
alter, altr	other	alternate, alternative, alter ego, altruism
ama, ami	love	amateur, amiable, amicable, amorous
ambul	walk	amble, ambulatory, somnambulist, perambulator
angle, angul	corner	angle, rectangle, quadrangle, triangular
annus	year	anniversary, annual, biannual, annuity
anthropo	man, humankind	anthropology, misanthrope, philanthropist, anthropopathism
aqua	water	aquarium, aquatic, aquamarine, aqueduct
arch	chief	architect, monarch, archbishop, hierarchy
arch, arche	ancient, first	archaeology, archaic, archive, archetype
arm	weapon	armor, armory, armistice, armada
aster, astro	star	asterisk, disaster, astronomy, astronaut
athl, athlon	prize, contest	athlete, athletic, decathlon, pentathlon
aud	hear	auditorium, audience, audition, audible
auto	self	autobiography, autocracy, autonomy, autograph
avi	bird	aviator, aviary, aviculture, avicide
baro	weight	barometer, barograph, baroscope, isobar
belli	war	belligerent, bellicose, post-bellum, ante-bellum
bene	good, well	benediction, benefit, beneficiary
bibl	book	Bible, Biblical, bibliography, bibliophile
bio	life	biology, biography, biopsy, antibiotic
brev	short	brevity, breviary, abbreviate, breve
bronch	windpipe	bronchitis, bronchial, bronchotomy, bronchopneumonia
bursa	bag, purse	bursar, bursitis, reimburse, disburse
camera	vault, chamber	bicameral, camera, unicameral, cameral
cand	glow, white, pure	candle, candidate, candelabra, incandescent
cant	song	canto, incantation, canticle, cantor
cap	head	cap, captain, capital (city), decapitate

ROOT	MEANING	SAMPLE WORDS
capt	take, receive	capture, captivity, captivate, captor
cardi	heart	electrocardiogram, cardiac, cardiograph, cardiectomy
carn	flesh	chili con carne, incarnation, carnivorous, carnal
cav	hollow	cave, cavern, concave, excavate
ced, ceed	go, yield	precede, recede, accede, antecedent
cens	judge	censor, censorship, census, censure
cept	take, receive, catch	reception, conception, accept, receptive
choreia, chorus	dancing	choreography, chorus, chorister, Terpsichore
chron	time	anachronism, chronicle, chronic, chronological
cide	kill	suicide, fratricide, herbicide, genocide
circ	ring, around	circle, circus, circuitous, circuit
civ	citizen	civilization, civil, civility, civic
claim	shout	acclaim, exclaim, declaim, proclaim
clam	shout	exclamation, proclamation, acclamation, clamor
clar	clear	clarify, declarative, declaration, clarity
class	class, group	classify, classical, classic, declassify
clin	lean	declination, decline, recline, incline
clud	shut	include, preclude, exclude, seclude
clus	shut	conclusive, exclusive, seclusion, inclusion
cogn	know	recognize, cognitive, cognizant, incognito
colo, cult	cultivate, settle	colony, agriculture, culture, cultivate
commun	common	community, commune, communicate, communicable
cornu	horn	unicorn, cornucopia, bicorn, cornet
corp	body	corporation, corps, corpuscle, corpulent
cosm	order, universe	cosmopolitan, microcosm, cosmos, macrocosm
cracy, crat	rule	aristocracy, democratic, bureaucrat, plutocrat
cred	believe	creditor, credulous, credentials, credibility
crim	judge, accuse	crime, criminal, incriminate, discriminate
crit	separate, judge	critic, criticize, criterion, critical
crypt	secret	cryptic, crypt, cryptogram, cryptography
culp	fault, blame	culpable, exculpate, culprit, inculpate
cum	pile up	accumulate, cumulative, cumulate, cumulus
cumb, cub	lie, recline	incubate, incumbent, succumb, incumbency
cur, cour	run	course, courier, current, excursion
cur	care	cure, manicure, accurate, curator

ROOT	MEANING	SAMPLE WORDS
cycl	ring, circle	bicycle, cyclic, cyclone, cyclist
dat	give	data, postdate, mandate, antedate
deb	owe	debt, indebted, debtor, debit
decor	proper, fitting	decoration, decor, indecorous, decorum
dei	god	deity, deify, deiform, deism
demos	people	democracy, epidemic, demography, demagogue
dent	tooth	dentist, dental, dentifrice, trident
derm	skin	hypodermic, dermatology, dermatitis, epidermis
dia, die	day	diary, per diem, sine die, dismal
dic, dict	say	dictate, predict, verdict, contradict
dign	worth	dignity, dignitary, condign, dignify
div	separate	divide, divisor, divisive, dividend
do	give	donate, donor, condone, donee
doc	teach	doctor, doctrine, indoctrinate, documentary
dorm	sleep	dormitory, dormant, dormer, dormancy
doxa	belief, praise	unorthodox, heterodoxy, orthodoxy, paradox
duc	lead	conduct, abduct, aqueduct, seduce
dur	hard	durable, endurable, endure, duress
dyn	power	dynamite, dynamic, dynasty, dynamo
ego	I	egotistic, ego, egocentric, egomania
em, empt	buy, obtain	exempt, caveat emptor, redemption, preempt
emia, hemia	blood	anemia, leukemia, hemostat, hemorrhage
enni	year	biennial, centennial, perennial, bicentennial
equ	equal, even, just	equality, equator, inequity, equation
erg	work	energy, erg, anergy, synergy
err	wander	err, error, erratic, erroneous
esth	feeling	esthetic, anesthetic, esthete, anesthetist
fac	make, do	manufacture, factory, benefactor, facsimile
fall, fals	deceive	fallacy, infallible, falsify, false
femina	woman	female, feminine, feminist, effeminate
fer	carry, bear	transfer, refer, infer, melliferous
fic	do, make	efficient, beneficial, sufficient, proficient
fid	faith	confide, fidelity, infidel, bona fide
fili	son, daughter	filial, affiliate, filicide, affiliation
fin	end	final, finite, infinite, finale
firm	steady	confirm, infirm, affirm, confirmation
fix	fasten	suffix, affix, fixture, prefix
flam	blaze	flame, inflammable, flammable, flamboyant

ROOT	MEANING	SAMPLE WORDS
flect	bend	reflect, reflector, deflect, inflection
flex	bend	reflex, flexible, flex, circumflex
flor	flower	flora, floral, efflorescent, florist
flu	flow	fluid, fluent, influx, affluent
fol	leaf	portfolio, foliage, folio, defoliate
form	shape	uniform, reform, formation, transform
fort	strong	fort, fortify, fortification, fortitude
fract, frag	break	fraction, fracture, fragment, fragile
frat	brother	fraternity, fraternal, fraternize, fratricide
fru	enjoy	fruit, fruitful, fructify, fruition
fug	flee	fugitive, refuge, refugee, centrifugal
funct	perform	functional, malfunction, defunct, dysfunction
fus	pour	transfusion, fusion, diffuse, profuse
gam	marriage	monogamy, bigamy, trigamy, polygamy
gen	race, birth	generation, progeny, genetics, genocide
geo	earth	geography, geology, apogee, perigee
gnos	know	agnostic, diagnose, diagnostic, prognosticate
gon	angle	trigonometry, octagonal, polygon, pentagon
grad	step	degrade, graduation, gradation, retrograde
gram	letter, written	monogram, telegram, grammar, epigram
gran	grain	grain, granary, grange, granulated
graph	write	autograph, paragraph, graphite, biography
grat	please, thank	grateful, congratulate, gratis, gratitude
greg	herd	congregation, gregarious, aggregate, desegregate
gyn	woman	monogyny, polygyny, gynecologist, misogynist
hedr	side, seat	polyhedron, tetrahedron, cathedral, ex cathedra
heli	sun	helium, heliotrope, heliocentric, heliograph
hom	man	homage, homo sapiens, homicide, hombre
homo	same	homogenized, homonym, homograph, homophone
hum	earth, soil	humus, humiliate, exhume, inhume
hydr	water	hydrant, hydrogen, hydrophobia, dehydrate
iatrik, iatro	healing art	pediatrician, psychiatric, geriatrics, podiatry
ident	same	identify, identical, identification, identity
idio	peculiar	idiot, idiom, idiomatic, idiosyncrasy
ign	fire	ignite, ignition, igneous, ignitron
imperi	command	imperative, empire, emperor, imperious
insul	island	peninsula, insulate, insularity, insular

ROOT	MEANING	SAMPLE WORDS
integ	whole, untouched	integrity, integrate, integral, integer
ir	anger	irritate, irate, ire, irascible
it	go	exit, initiate, adit, obit
ject	throw	project, inject, reject, eject
jocus	joke	joke, jocose, jocular, jocund
journ	daily	journal, journalism, journey, sojourn
ju, jud	law, right	judge, judicial, judgment, judicious
junct	join	junction, conjunction, juncture, adjunct
jur	law, right	jury, perjury, jurisdiction, jurisprudence
jus	law, right	just, justice, injustice, justification
labor	work	collaborate, laboratory, elaborate, laborious
laps	slip	elapse, relapse, lapse, collapse
lat	side	lateral, unilateral, bilateral, quadrilateral
lect	gather, choose	collect, elect, select, electoral
lect, leg	read	lectern, legend, legible, illegible
leg	law, contract	legal, delegate, legitimate, legislate
lev	raise, lift	elevator, leverage, lever, levee
liber	free	liberty, liberate, libertarian, liberal
libr	book	library, librarian, librettist, libretto
lingu	tongue	lingual, linguistics, linguist, bilingual
litera	letter	literature, literary, illiterate, literal
lith	stone	monolith, paleolithic, neolithic, lithograph
loc	place	local, location, dislocate, localize
locu	speak	locution, elocution, circumlocution, interlocutor
log, logue, logy	speech	dialogue, prologue, epilogue, eulogy
lop	run, leap	elope, interloper, elopement, lope
loqu	speak	eloquence, soliloquy, colloquial, loquacious
lu	wash	deluge, antediluvian, ablution, dilute
luc	light	lucid, translucent, elucidate, Lucifer
lud	play	interlude, prelude, postlude, ludicrous
luna	moon	lunar, lunatic, translunar, cislunar
magni	great	magnify, magnitude, magnanimity, magnificent
mal	bad	malice, malady, malign, malignant
man	hand	manual, manuscript, manipulate, manicure
mand	order	command, demand, mandatory, mandate
mare	sea	marine, submarine, mariner, maritime

ROOT	MEANING	SAMPLE WORDS
mater, matri	mother, source	maternal, maternity, alma mater, matron
med	middle	medium, mediate, medieval, mediocre
memoria	memory	commemorate, memorize, memorandum, memorial
ment	mind	mental, demented, mentality, memento
merg	plunge, dip	merge, submerge, merger, emerge
meter	measure	diameter, barometer, altimeter, perimeter
metr	measure	metric, geometric, isometric, symmetrical
migr	move	migrate, emigrate, immigrant, migratory
mil	soldier	militant, military, militia, militate
mim	imitate	mimic, mimeograph, pantomime, mime
miser	wretched, pity	miserable, miser, misery, commiserate
miss	send, let go	mission, missionary, missive, missile
mnem	memory	amnesia, mnemonic, amnesty, Mnemosyne
mob	move	automobile, mobile, immobile, mobility
mon	advise, warn	admonish, monitor, admonition, premonition
mor	custom	moral, morality, morals, mores
mort	death	mortal, immortal, mortality, mortician
mot	move	motion, motor, promote, demote
mov	move	move, movable, remove, movie
mut	change, exchange	mutual, commute, mutuality, mutation
nat	born	native, nativity, natal, innate
naus, naut	ship	nausea, nautical, nautilus, aquanaut
nav	ship	navy, navigate, naval, circumnavigate
nes	island	Indonesia, Polynesian, Micronesia, Dodecanese
nom	law, arrangement	astronomy, economy, autonomy, taxonomy
nomen	name	nomenclature, denomination, nominative, nominate
nov	new	novel, novelty, novice, innovate
numer	number	numeral, numerator, numerous, enumerate
ocul	eye	ocular, oculist, binoculars, monocular
onym	name	antonym, synonym, homonym, acronym
op, opt	sight	myopic, optic, optometrist, optical
orare	speak, pray	oral, oracle, orator, oratory
oss, osteo	bone	ossify, osteopath, osteomyelitis, osteotomy
ov	egg	oval, ovum, ovary, oviparous
paed, ped	child, teach	encyclopedia, pedantic, pedagogue, pediatrician

ROOT	MEANING	SAMPLE WORDS
par	give birth	parent, parentage, biparous, viviparous
par	equal, compare	compare, comparable, parable, parity
past	shepherd	pastor, pastoral, pastorale, pasture
pater, patr	father	paternal, patriarch, patriot, repatriation
path	feel, suffer	sympathy, empathy, pathos, antipathy
ped	foot	pedal, pedestrian, biped, centipede
pel	drive	repel, dispel, expel, propel
pen, pun	punishment	penal, penitentiary, penalize, punitive
pend, pens	hang	pendulum, appendage, suspend, appendix
petr	rock	petrify, petroleum, petrification, petrol
phag	eat	esophagus, dysphagia, sarcophagous, anthropophagi
phil	love	philharmonic, philosopher, philatelist, Philadelphia
phobos	fear	Phobos, agoraphobia, claustrophobia, acrophobia
phon	sound	phone, symphony, phonics, telephone
phor	to carry	euphoria, dysphoria, metaphor, semaphore
photo	light	photocell, photosynthesis, photography, photostatic
plac	please	placate, placid, complacent, placebo
pne	air, lung, breathe	pneumatic, pneumonia, apnea, pneumonoultramicroscopicsilicovolcanoconiosis
pod, pus	foot	bipod, tripod, chiropodist, octopus
poli, polit	city	acropolis, metropolis, politics, politician
port	carry	transport, import, export, deport
porta	gate	port, seaport, portal, Puerto [Porto] Rico
pos	place, set	depose, deposit, preposition, apposition
pter	wing, feather	helicopter, pterodactyl, pterosaur, lepidopterous
puls	drive, push	repulse, expulsion, compulsory, propulsion
quer, quest, quir	seek, ask	query, questionnaire, inquest, inquire
rect	straight, right	correct, rectify, erect, rectangle
referre	carry back	refer, reference, referendum, referent
reg, regn	rule	regal, regime, regency, interregnum
rid, ris	laugh	deride, ridiculous, ridicule, derision
rod, ros	gnaw	rodent, erode, corrode, erosion
rogare	ask, request	interrogate, interrogative, prerogative, abrogate
rota	wheel, round	rotate, rotary, rotunda, rotor
rupt	to break	rupture, erupt, interrupt, disrupt
sacr	holy	sacrifice, sacrament, sacred, sacrilege

ROOT	MEANING	SAMPLE WORDS
san	healthy, sound	sane, sanity, sanitation, sanitarium
sanct	holy	sanctuary, sanctity, sanctify, sanctimonious
sat, satis	enough	satiety, saturate, insatiable, satisfy
saur	lizard	dinosaur, tyrannosaurus, sauropod, brontosaurus
scend, scens	climb	descend, ascend, transcend, ascension
schole	leisure, school	school, scholastic, scholarship, scholar
sci	know	science, conscious, scientific, omniscient
scope	to watch	telescope, microscope, periscope, kaleidoscope
scrib, script	write	describe, inscribe, manuscript, inscription
sec, sect	cut	dissect, bisect, insect, intersect
sed, sess, sid	sit, settle	sedative, sedentary, session, preside
semin	seed	seminary, disseminate, seminarian, seminar
sen	old	senator, senior, seniority, senile
sens, sent	feel	sensitive, sensation, assent, dissent
seps, sept	decay	antiseptic, septic, aseptic, septicemia
sequ	follow	sequence, subsequent, sequel, consequently
serv	save, keep	reservoir, reservation, preservation, conservation
servus	slave, server	service, servitude, subservient, servile
sexus	division, sex	sex, sexual, sexism, bisexual
signi	mark, sign	signify, signal, signature, insignia
simil, simul	like, same	similarity, simile, simultaneous, simulate
sol	alone	solitude, solitary, desolate, soliloquy
solidus	solid	solid, solidarity, consolidate, solidify
solu, solv	loosen, free	soluble, dissolve, solvent, absolve
somn	sleep	insomnia, insomniac, somnambulist, somnolent
son	sound	unison, sonorous, dissonant, subsonic
soph	wise	philosopher, sophisticated, sophomoric, sophistry
spec, spect	look	spectator, spectacular, spectacle, prospect
spher	ball, sphere	atmosphere, hemisphere, stratosphere, spherical
spir	breathe, live	conspirator, inspire, respiration, expire
spond, spons	answer	respond, respondent, correspondent, responsive
sta	stand	stationary, standard, stability, stagnant
stru	build	construct, structure, instruct, structural
studeo	be eager	student, studious, study, studio
surg, surr	rise	surge, resurgence, resurrection, insurrection
syllaba	take together	syllable, syllabus, syllabify, syllabification

WORD STRUCTURE AND VOCABULARY

ROOT	MEANING	SAMPLE WORDS
tabl, tabula	board, tablet	table, tablet, entablature, tabular
tact, tang	touch	intact, tangent, tangible, intangible
tain, ten	hold	attain, retain, detain, tenacious
tact, tax	to arrange, order	tactics, syntactical, syntax, taxidermist
tele	distant	telephone, telegraph, telescope, television
temp	time, season	temporary, contemporary, temporal, extemporaneous
tend, tens, tent	tend, stretch	extend, tendon, tensile, extent
terrere	to frighten	terrify, terror, terrorist, terrible
testare	to witness	testify, testimony, testament, intestate
thanatos	death	thanatophobia, thanatopsis, euthanasia, Thanatos
the	god	theism, atheist, theology, monotheism
thermo	heat	thermos, thermometer, thermal, thermostat
tom	cut	appendectomy, tonsillectomy, neurectomy, anatomy
topos	place, spot	topical, topography, utopia, topology
tort	twist, turn	distort, extort, retort, torture
tox	poison	toxin, antitoxin, toxic, intoxication
tract	pull, draw, drag	attract, tractor, distract, extract
trud	thrust	intrude, protrude, extrude, obtrude
tuitus	watch over	tuition, tutorial, tutelage, tutor
turb	whirling, turmoil	turbine, turbid, turbulent, perturb
ultimus	last	antepenult, ultimate, penult, ultimatum
umber, umbra	shade, shadow	umbra, umbrella, adumbrate, penumbra
unda	wave	undulate, inundate, abundant, redundant
urb	city	urban, urbane, suburb, suburban
vaca, vacu	empty, hollow	vacate, vacant, vacuum, evacuate
vad, vas	go	invade, evade, pervade, evasive
vag	wander	vagrant, vagrancy, vagabond, extravagant
val	strong, worth	valid, equivalent, invalid, valetudinarian
van	front, forward	vanguard, van, avant-garde, vantage point
vapor	steam	vapor, vaporous, vaporizer, evaporate
vari	different, various, spotted	vary, variant, variety, variegated
ven	come	convention, convent, intervention, convene
ven	sale	vend, vendor, venal, caveat vendor

ROOT	MEANING	SAMPLE WORDS
ven	vein	vein, venous, intravenous, venule
ver	true	verdict, verify, veracity, verification
ver, verer	fear, awe	reverence, reverend, revere, irreverent
verb	word	verb, adverb, proverb, verbatim
vers, vert	turn	reverse, inverse, divert, invert
vesper	evening	vespers, Vesper, Hesperus, vespertilionid
vest	clothing	vest, vestment, divest, investiture
veter	old, experienced	vet, veteran, veterinary, veterinarian
via	way	viaduct, trivial, trivia, deviate
vict	conquer	victory, evict, victorious, victor
vid	see	video, providence, evident, videotape
vis	see	vision, visualize, visible, supervision
vit	live	vitamin, vitality, vital, revitalize
viv	live	survive, revive, vivid, vivacious
voc, voke	call	vocal, vocabulary, avocation, evoke
vol	wish, will	volunteer, benevolent, malevolent, involuntary
vol, volv	roll, turn	revolt, revolve, evolve, revolver
vor	eat	devour, voracious, carnivorous, herbivorous
zo	animal	zoo, zoologist, protozoan, zodiac

An *affix* is a syllable or syllables put at the beginning or end of a word or root to change its meaning. A *prefix* comes at the beginning of a word; a *suffix* comes at the end of a word. Following are lists of some of the most important prefixes and suffixes used in English.

2.B

Affixes

PREFIX	MEANING	SAMPLE WORDS
a-	on	ashore, aboard, afire, atop
a-, an-	not, without	atom, aseptic, anemia, anergy
ab-	from	absent, abduct, abdicate, abnormal
ad-	to	adhere, adjoin, adverb, adjunct
ambi-	both, around	ambidextrous, ambiguous, ambivalent, ambient
amphi-	both, around	amphibious, amphitheater, amphipod, amphora
ante-	before	anteroom, anterior, antecedent, antechamber
anti-	against	antifreeze, antidote, antislavery, antiseptic
apo-	away from, from	apogee, apostle, apostasy, apocryphal

PREFIX	MEANING	SAMPLE WORDS
auto-	self	autograph, automobile, automatic, autobiography
bene-	well, good	benefit, beneficial, benediction, benefactor
bi-, bin-, bis-	two, twice	bicycle, binocular, bigamy, biceps
cent-	hundred	century, centigrade, centimeter, centennial
circu-	around, about	circus, circuit, circa, circular
circum-	around	circumnavigate, circumpolar, circumference, circumlocution
co-	with, together	co-worker, cooperator, coincident, coalition
col-	together, with	collect, collaborate, collate, colleague
com-	together, with	companion, compost, compact, compose
con-	together, with	connect, concentrate, conference, congress
contra-, contro-	against	contrast, contradict, contrary, controversy
counter-	against, in return	counterclockwise, counteract, counterbalance, counterrevolution
de-	down	descend, degrade, depress, dejected
de-	away	deflect, deter, detract, dehydrate
dec-	ten	decade, decimal, December, decathlon
deci-	tenth	decimal, decimate, decibel, decimeter
demi-, hemi-, semi-	half, partly	demigod, hemidemisemiquaver, hemisphere, semiconscious
di-	two	diphthong, dioxide, digraph, dilemma
dia-	through, between	diameter, diagonal, dialogue, diagnosis
dis-	not	dishonest, distrustful, discontent, disobey
dis-	apart from	dismiss, discard, disarm, dislocate
dis-	opposite	disarrange, discomfort, disconnect, disown
du-	two	dual, duet, duplex, duplicate
dys-	bad	dyspepsia, dysfunction, dysentery, dystrophy
e-	out	eject, emit, erupt, elevate
en-	in	encircle, enfold, encase, enslave
endo-	inside, within	endoderm, endocrine, endocarp, endogamy
epi-	upon, in addition	epilogue, epidermis, epitaph, epidemic
eu-	well, good	eulogy, euphemism, euphoria, euphonious
ex-	out	exit, extract, exclude, excerpt
extra-	outside, beyond	extramural, extravagant, extraordinary, extradite
hept-, sept-	seven	heptagon, heptarchy, septennial, September

PREFIX	MEANING	SAMPLE WORDS
hetero-	different	heteronym, heterogeneous, heterodox, heterosexual
homo-	same	homonym, homogeneous, homogenesis, homologous
hyper-	over, beyond	hypersensitive, hyperbole, hyperacidity, hypertension
hypo-	under, too little	hypoactive, hypochondriac, hypodermic, hypotenuse
il-	not	illegal, illogical, illegible, illiterate
im-	into	immerse, immigrate, implant, impale
im-	not	immovable, immobile, immaculate, impartial
in-	into	intake, inhale, include, incision
in-	not	inactive, incorrect, indecent, informal
infra-	below	infrared, infrahuman, infraglacial, infrastructure
inter-	between, among	international, interurban, intermission, interjection
intra-, intro-	within	intramural, introduce, introvert, introspective
ir-	not	irregular, irreverent, irrational, irrelevant
iso-	equal, same	isobar, isometric, isotope, isosceles
kilo-	1,000	kilocycle, kilogram, kilometer, kilowatt
macro-	large, long	macron, macroscopic, macrometer, macrocosm
mega-	large	megalomania, megaphone, megalith, megaton
meta-	change	metaphor, metamorphic, metabolism, metastasis
meta-	beyond	metaphysics, metapsychosis, metabiological, metachrome
micro-	small	microscopic, microphone, micrometer, microfilm
milli-	1/1,000	millimeter, milligram, millisecond, milliwatt
mis-	wrong	misspell, misdeed, misinterpret, misbehave
mono-	one	monarch, monocle, monorail, monotone
multi-	many	multitude, multimillionaire, multicolored, multilateral
neo-	new, modern	neologism, neophyte, neolithic, neonate
non-	not	nonstop, nonsense, nonentity, nonpolitical
non-, novem-	nine	nonagon, November, novena, novennial
ob-	against, opposite	objection, obstacle, obstruct, obverse
octa-, octo-	eight	octagon, octopus, October, octogenarian
olig-	few	oligarchy, oligopoly, oligochrome, oligocarpous
omni-	all	omnipotent, omnivorous, omniscient, omnibus

PREFIX	MEANING	SAMPLE WORDS
pan-	all	pandemonium, Pan-American, pandemic, panorama
para-	beside	paragraph, parallel, parasite, paraphrase
pen-, pene-	almost	peninsula, penannular, penultimate, peneplain
penta-	five	pentagon, Pentecost, pentameter, pentad
per-	throughout, thoroughly	pervade, perpetual, permanent, perforate
peri-	around, near, about	periscope, perimeter, periphery, perigee
poly-	many	polygon, polysyllable, polygamy, polytheism
post-	after	postscript, postpone, postdate, posterity
pre-	before	predict, presume, precede, premeditate
pro-	before	prognosis, program, progenitor, prophesy
pro-	in place of	pronoun, pronominal, proconsul, proconsulate
pro-	forward	project, propel, progress, promenade
pro-	in favor of	proslavery, pro-American, pro-liberal, proponent
pro-	in front	prologue, proboscis, program, proseminar
proto-	first	protozoa, prototype, protoplasm, protocol
pseudo-	false	pseudonym, pseudopod, pseudo-event, pseudoscience
quad-, quart-, quatr-	four	quadruplet, quadruped, quarter, quatrain
quasi-	seemingly, partly, as if	quasi-humorous, quasi-historical, quasi-judicial, quasi-legislative
quin-	five	quintet, quintuplet, quintuple, quintessence
re-	back	refund, retract, repay, remit
re-	again	reread, rearrange, rediscover, reabsorb
retro-	back	retrorocket, retroactive, retrograde, retrospection
semi-	half	semicircle, semiannual, semiconscious, semifinals
sept-	seven	September, septennial, septet, septuagenarian
sesqui-	one and a half	sesquilateral, sesquicentennial, sesquioxide, sesquipedalian
sex-, hex-	six	sextet, sextuplet, hexagonal, hexameter
sub-	under, below	submarine, subsoil, submerge, subterranean
super-	over	supersede, supernatural, superheat, supercilious
sym-	together, with	sympathy, symphony, symmetry, symposium
syn-	together, with	synonym, synthesis, synopsis, synchronous
tetra-	four	tetragonal, tetrameter, tetrarchy, tetrachloride
trans-	across, over	transfer, transmit, transit, transcontinental

PREFIX	MEANING	SAMPLE WORDS
tri-	three	triangle, tricycle, trigonometry, triad
ultra-	beyond	ultraviolet, ultramodern, ultranationalism, ultrasonic
un-	not	unsafe, unsure, unreliable, unmanned
uni-	one	unit, unicycle, unify, unique
vice-	in place of	vice-president, vice-principal, vice-admiral, viceroy

SUFFIX	MEANING	SAMPLE WORDS
-able, -ble, -ible	can be done	eatable, lovable, readable, credible
-able, -ble, -ible	inclined to	peaceable, perishable, affordable, durable
-acy, -cy	office, rank of, state of	candidacy, privacy, infancy, agency
-ade	result, product, substance made	orangeade, lemonade, limeade, marmalade
-ade	process, action	parade, blockade, escapade, promenade
-ae	Latin feminine plural	alumnae, formulae, algae, larvae
-age	place of	orphanage, parsonage, anchorage, frontage
-age	action, process	ravage, pillage, marriage, pilgrimage
-al	relating to	filial, natural, ornamental, royal
-an	relating to	veteran, American, Anglican, European
-ance	state of	resistance, avoidance, importance, exuberance
-ancy	state of	vacancy, truancy, occupancy, ascendancy
-and, -end	to be done	multiplicand, addend, dividend, subtrahend
-ant	state of, condition of	defiant, radiant, vacant, buoyant
-ant, -ent	person who	immigrant, emigrant, assistant, resident
-arian	person who, place where, object which	grammarian, librarian, humanitarian, libertarian
-ary	person who, place where, object which	secretary, sanctuary, dictionary, infirmary
-ary	characterized by, relating to	literary, military, reactionary, secondary
-ate	to make, cause to be	annihilate, liberate, radiate, venerate

SUFFIX	MEANING	SAMPLE WORDS
-ation	process, action	narration, continuation, visitation, computation
-ation	state of, quality of, result of	occupation, moderation, decoration, refrigeration
-atory	process, action, place where	oratory, reformatory, laboratory, conservatory
-cule	small	minuscule, molecule, animalcule, pedicule
-dom	state of	freedom, martyrdom, wisdom, boredom
-ectomy	surgical removal	tonsillectomy, gastrectomy, appendectomy, hysterectomy
-en	to make	lengthen, shorten, weaken, strengthen
-ence	state, quality, condition of	dependence, confidence, competence, absence
-ency	quality of, state of	potency, despondency, clemency, frequency
-er	comparative degree	faster, lighter, clearer, tighter
-er, -or	person connected with	carpenter, barber, actor, orator
-ery, -ry	place where	bakery, rookery, bindery, laundry
-ese	derivation, language	Japanese, Maltese, Chinese, Nepalese
-esque	in the manner, style of, like	picturesque, burlesque, Romanesque, statuesque
-ess	feminine ending	actress, shepherdess, countess
-et, -ette	small	islet, dinette, kitchenette, statuette
-eur	agent	amateur, chauffeur, masseur, saboteur
-ful	enough to fill	cupful, spoonful, mouthful, handful
-fy	make of, form into	satisfy, amplify, deify, qualify
-hood	state of, quality of, condition of	knighthood, manhood, falsehood, womanhood
-ial	characterized by, related to	connubial, industrial, commercial, remedial
-ian	characterized by, related to	Christian, physician, Parisian, barbarian
-ic	of the nature of, characterized by	angelic, iambic, volcanic, quixotic
-ic	to form nouns	magic, classic, public, rhetoric

SUFFIX	MEANING	SAMPLE WORDS
-ical	of the nature of, characterized by	critical, fantastical, comical, political
-icle	little	canticle, particle, article, icicle
-ier, -yer	person who, place where	cashier, gondolier, chiffonier, lawyer
-ine	like, characterized by, pertaining to	canine, feline, asinine, feminine
-ine	feminine suffix	heroine, Caroline, Josephine, Clementine
-ing	present participle	sleeping, walking, writing, acting
-ing	material	roofing, bedding, siding, quilting
-ings	noun associated with the verb form	earnings, shavings, furnishings, filings
-ion	act, process	construction, rebellion, revolution, electrocution
-ion	state of	ambition, dominion, subjection, suspicion
-ious	characterized by	gracious, ambitious, infectious, dubious
-ise, -ize	subject to, make, carry on	exorcise, baptize, sterilize, civilize
-ish	like, pertaining to	Scottish, Turkish, clownish, whitish
-ism	action, process	baptism, plagiarism, despotism, heroism
-ism	state of, condition of	hypnotism, barbarism, racism, pacifism
-ism	doctrine, system	stoicism, Quakerism, Americanism, realism
-ist	person who	biologist, monopolist, botanist, socialist
-itis	inflammatory disease	appendicitis, bronchitis, arthritis, meningitis
-ity	state of	calamity, felicity, necessity, acidity
-less	without	witless, fruitless, doubtless, careless
-let	small	streamlet, ringlet, leaflet, bracelet
-like	like	homelike, lifelike, apelike, ghostlike
-ling	small	duckling, gosling, hireling, nestling
-logy	science of	anthropology, biology, zoology, psychology
-ly	characteristic of, in the manner of	fatherly, motherly, regally, timely

SUFFIX	MEANING	SAMPLE WORDS
-ment	action, process	development, abridgment, government, embezzlement
-ment	state of	amazement, adornment, arrangement, refinement
-ness	state of, quality of, condition of	greatness, kindness, wilderness, dimness
-oid	like, resembling	adenoid, asteroid, spheroid, planetoid
-or	person who	auditor, donor, creditor, executor
-orium	place for, object used for	auditorium, natatorium, emporium, conservatorium
-ory	place where	laboratory, conservatory, consistory, purgatory
-osis	abnormal condition, state of	hypnosis, psychosis, neurosis, otiosis
-ous	possessing the qualities of	poisonous, riotous, joyous, polygamous
-ry	collection of	jewelry, revelry, masonry, citizenry
-ship	state of	hardship, friendship, censorship, ownership
-ship	office, profession	clerkship, lordship, authorship, partnership
-ship	art, skill	stewardship, scholarship, penmanship, horsemanship
-ster	one belonging to, characterized by	mobster, gangster, huckster, youngster
-ule	little, small	capsule, molecule, plumule, tubule
-wise	way, manner, respect	clockwise, counterclockwise, lengthwise, slantwise

2.C

Synonyms and Antonyms

A *synonym* is a word that means about the same as another word.

Walk, hike, stroll, stride, tramp, march, roam, pace, ramble, amble, meander, saunter, and *promenade* are synonyms.

Sometimes one synonym will be more appropriate than another. *See* **2.E**: Denotation and Connotation *and* **2.G**: Using a Dictionary.

An *antonym* is a word that means the opposite of another word.

Wet and *dry, hot* and *cold,* and *forward* and *backward* are antonym pairs.

Context clues are hints to the meaning of a particular word that are given in the surrounding sentence or paragraph.

Sometimes the way the word is used provides a clue to its meaning. *See* **4.A**: Parts of Speech *and* **4.B**: Parts of a Sentence.

Other times the context may actually define the word. Following are some of the ways a word may be defined within its context.

Context Clues

Formal Definition. This clue is usually a direct statement that defines the word for you.

An oyster is a *sea animal with a soft body inside a hard, two-piece shell.*

Definition by Example. The clue is an example included to help you.

Erosion wears away the earth. *Running water, for example, carries loose soil, sand, gravel, and boulders and then deposits them in new places.*

Definition by Description. Here, the description of a word helps you visualize that word.

The saber-toothed tiger was a *catlike prehistoric animal with long, pointed teeth near the front of its mouth. The teeth were shaped like sabers.*

Definition by Simile. *Simile* is a Latin word meaning "like" or "similar." In a phrase beginning with *like* or *as,* the simile gives you a context clue by comparing a word with something else.

Badminton is a game somewhat *like tennis.*

Definition by Comparison and Contrast. This context clue compares and contrasts a word in greater detail than a simile.

Badminton is a game somewhat like tennis. *But the shuttlecock (made of feather and cork) must be hit back and forth over the net without hitting the ground.*

Definition by Appositive. An appositive explains or identifies a noun in the sentence. Commas usually set off this clue.

Schussing, *skiing straight down a slope without turning or stopping,* is the fastest form of skiing.

Definition by Origin. This explanation consists of information about the language in which the word originated.

Do you know the drink of the gods? It's an *ancient Greek word we still use today: nectar.*

Parenthetical Definition. This clue is in parentheses.

Amphetamine drugs may cause people to hallucinate *(see, hear, or feel stimuli that are not present).*

Indirect Definition. Writers often define words indirectly. Look for signal words such as *called, also called, or, known as, referred to,* and *that is.* This type of clue is sometimes italicized.

Cameras control the amount of light passing through the lens with changeable openings called *stops.*

NOTE: An *idiom* is a phrase whose total meaning is different from the meaning of the individual words. Idioms cannot be interpreted literally, word-by-word. Since they come from language usage, they must be learned as new vocabulary words are learned.

cut it out   eat your words   fall flat   button your lip

If there is enough surrounding context, you may have a clue to the meaning of an idiom. At other times you will know you are dealing with an idiom only because the literal interpretation simply does not make sense.

She *blew her top.* (No context.)
She *blew her top* when someone stepped in front of her in line after she'd been waiting twenty minutes.
(Context tells you that she was probably very angry because someone stepped in front of her.)

If there is not enough context to determine the meaning of an idiom, look up the key word of the expression in a dictionary.

The *denotation* of a word is its dictionary, or lexical, meaning. The denotations of some words are more specific and definite than the denotations of others.

Denotation and Connotation

Concrete words are words that have a core of meaning for anyone who reads or speaks them. Proper names (names of people and places) are the most concrete, or specific, words of all.

Relative words are words that are descriptive and have shades of meaning.

> *Red* may be pinkish red, orangy red, or purplish red. In a family where the tallest member is 5′6″, a person 5′10″ is *tall*. If the shortest person in another family is 5′10″, someone 5′10″ is not *tall*.

Abstract words are words that do not refer to specific objects. They have definite meaning only because of their accepted usage.

> The words *labor, culture, education,* and *art* mean different things to different people.

The *connotation* of a word is the complex of ideas and emotions that the word evokes. These connotations may be positive, negative, or neutral.

Positive Connotation	Neutral Connotation	Negative Connotation
famous	well-known	notorious
slender	thin	skinny
	average	mediocre
fluent	talkative	garrulous

Figures of Speech

A *figure of speech* is a word or phrase used in an imaginative rather than a literal way. Figurative language may be used to show comparison, contrast, or association.

2.F.1 Figurative Comparisons

A *simile* is a comparison between two different things and is introduced by the words *like* or *as*. The objects compared are different in most respects, but for the writer's or speaker's purpose have one striking resemblance.

> He ate *like a pig.*

A *metaphor* makes a comparison between two different things without using *like* or *as*. It is a word taken from one context and used in another.

He was a pig at the table.

An *analogy* extends and elaborates on the implied or expressed comparisons of the metaphor or simile.

Education is *like a game in which more than one person takes part and each person has a position to play.* Your teachers are responsible for *the game plan*, and you are largely responsible for learning.

2.F.2 Figurative Contrasts

Hyperbole is an exaggeration used to emphasize or intensify a situation.

I told you *a million times* to close the refrigerator door.

Litotes are a type of understatement in which the writer or speaker uses the negative form of what is really meant.

Mom's *not a bad* cook. (Meaning: Mom's a great cook.)

Irony is an expression that implies the opposite of what is actually said.

He's a *terrible athlete*—he *only* holds one or two school records in each of the four major sports.

2.F.3 Figurative Associations

In *metonymy*, something that is closely associated with a second thing takes the place of the second thing's name.

The *White House* announced a press conference. (Meaning: the President or the President's staff announced the conference.)

Synecdoche is a figure of speech that names a part when the whole is meant. It may also name the whole when a part is meant.

The rancher hired six more *hands* for the roundup.
Chicago won the Stanley Cup.

Using a Dictionary

The word *dictionary* is from Latin *dictionarium*, related to *dicere* (say). The word *diction* means "speech" or "word." A dictionary explains the many words of a language.

Dictionary entry elements include:

- spelling
- syllabication
- pronunciation
- parts of speech, common and proper nouns
- definitions
- inflections (changes in a word, such as stead*y* and steadi*er*)
- cross-references
- abbreviations and symbols
- illustrations
- punctuation
- synonyms (words that mean the same or almost the same)
- antonyms (words that mean the opposite)
- homophones (words that sound the same)
- homographs (words spelled alike but having different meanings, origins, and, sometimes, pronunciations)
- word usage
- idioms (phrases peculiar to a language, such as *lend a hand*)
- foreign terms and phrases
- word origins (for example, the word *volt* is named after the Italian physicist Alessandro Volta)
- coined, or made-up, words
- slang
- etymology (word derivation)
- neologisms (new words or new meanings for old words)
- archaisms (out-of-date words, such as *methinks*)
- figures of speech (expressions in which words are used out of their literal meaning or in striking combinations to add beauty or force)
- historical and literary allusions or references (for example, the entry for *armada,* meaning "a fleet of warships," will refer you to the famous Armada, the Spanish fleet England defeated in 1588)

SAMPLE DICTIONARY ENTRIES

Word Entries begin in bold black type. Only proper nouns are capitalized. The first letter of the entry extends into the margin for easy location. This dictionary uses an asterisk to indicate that the entry is accompanied by an illustration.

Illustrations clarify the definitions. Labels show which meaning of the word is illustrated.

Pronunciations are given in phonetic symbols. This dictionary has a key to its phonetic symbols at the bottom of each right-hand page, with more detailed information at the front of the book.

Parts of Speech Labels show the word's grammatical use. Any word used as more than one part of speech is defined accordingly. The parts of speech are abbreviated, as in *adj.* for adjective and *n.* for *noun*. Verbs are shown as transitive (*v.t.*) or intransitive (*v.i.*).

Phrases that include the key word but have special meanings of their own are explained separately.

Synonyms that have the same or nearly the same meaning as the defined words appear immediately after the definition.

Synonym Studies explain in detail the various shades of meaning of some synonyms. All these studies include examples.

Usage Notes explain points of spelling or grammar and advise how to use the word in speaking or writing.

✱ ab|do|men (ab′də mən, ab dō′-), *n.* **1a** the part of the body containing the stomach and the intestines; belly. In man and other mammals the abdomen is a large cavity between the chest (thorax) and the pelvis, and also contains the liver, pancreas, kidneys, and spleen. **b** a corresponding region in vertebrates below mammals. **2** the last of the three parts of the body of insects and many other arthropods, including spiders and crustaceans. [< Latin *abdōmen*]

✱ **abdomen**
definition 2

abdomen   thorax   head

ab|dom|i|nal (ab dom′ə nəl), *adj.* of the abdomen; in the abdomen; for the abdomen: *Bending the body exercises the abdominal muscles.* **SYN:** ventral, visceral. — **ab|dom′i|nal|ly,** *adv.*
abdominal brain, = solar plexus.
ab|dom|i|nous (ab dom′ə nəs), *adj.* = potbellied.

a|bide¹ (ə bīd′), *v.*, **a|bode** or **a|bid|ed, a|bid|ing.**
— *v.t.* **1** to put up with; endure; tolerate: *A good housekeeper can't abide dust. She can't abide him.* **SYN:** bear, stand. **2** to await submissively; submit to; sustain: *He must abide his fatal doom* (Joanna Baillie). **3** to await defiantly; withstand: *He soon learned to abide ... terrors which most of my bolder companions shrank from encountering* (Hugh Miller). **4** *Archaic.* to wait for; await: *I will abide the coming of my lord* (Tennyson).
— *v.i.* **1** to stay; remain; wait: *Abide with me for a time. I'll call upon you straight: abide within* (Shakespeare). *He within his ships abode the while* (William Cowper). **2** to continue to live (in a place); reside; dwell: *No martin there in winter shall abide* (John Dryden). **3** to continue (in some state or action): *... ye shall abide in my love* (John 15:10). **4** to continue in existence; endure: *Thou hast established the earth, and it abideth* (Psalms 119:90). **SYN:** last. **5** *Archaic.* to be left. **6** *Obsolete.* to stay behind.
abide by, a to accept and follow out; be bound by: *Both teams will abide by the umpire's decision.* **b** to remain faithful to; stand firm by; be true to; fulfill: *Abide by your promise.*

a|bil|i|ty (ə bil′ə tē), *n., pl.* **-ties. 1** the power to do or act: *the ability to think clearly. The old horse still has the ability to work.* **SYN:** capability, capacity. **2** skill: *Washington had great ability as a general.* **3** power to do some special thing; natural gift; talent: *Musical ability often shows itself early in life.* [< Middle French *habilité,* learned borrowing from Latin *habilitās* aptness < *habilis* able]
— **Syn. 2, 3 Ability, talent** mean special power to do or for doing something. **Ability** applies to a demonstrated physical or mental power to do a certain thing well: *She has developed unusual ability as a dancer.* **Talent** applies to an inborn capacity for doing a special thing: *a child with a remarkable talent for painting.*
▶ After **ability** the infinitive of a verb preceded by *to* is used, rather than the gerund preceded by *of: A lawyer needs the ability to think clearly,* not *of thinking clearly.* The preposition used after *ability* and before a noun is *in: ability in music.*

A|bim|e|lech (ə bim′ə lek), *n.* a son of Gideon who was set up as king of Israel by the people of Shechem (in the Bible, Judges 9).
ab init., ab initio.
ab in|i|ti|o (ab′ i nish′ē ō), *Latin.* from the beginning: *The decree was not a nullity in the sense of being void ab initio* (London Times).

Definitions give the precise meanings of words. If a word has more than one meaning, the definitions are numbered. This dictionary lists the most common meanings first. Some dictionaries present definitions in historical order, with the earliest meanings first.

Examples point out how the word is used in phrases or sentences.

Cross-References show that the form consulted is less widely used than some other form, which has its own main entry.

Other Forms of the word include the principal parts of verbs, unusual plural forms, and comparative forms for adjectives.

Quotations from well-known authors or publications illustrate the meaning of the word. The sources of quotations are identified.

Levels of Usage Labels, such as *Slang, Informal, Archaic,* and *Obsolete,* indicate when and where the word is acceptable in current English usage. Each label is defined in a list at the front of the dictionary.

Derivations tell what language or languages a word comes from, usually with its meaning in the original language. The symbol < means comes from.

Foreign Words and Phrases in common use in English have entries that give their pronunciation and translation, often with examples or illustrative quotations.

From *The World Book Dictionary.*

The words explained in a dictionary are listed in alphabetical order, letter by letter. Pairs of guide words are usually at the top of a page or at the top of each set of facing pages. *Guide words* list the first and last defined word to appear on a page (or facing pages). Using guide words can help you quickly locate the word you seek.

> If the guide words on facing pages are *symbolic* and *sympathy,* you will have to turn to the next page to find *symphonic.*

**2.G.1
Guide Words**

Main entries are the words that are explained in a dictionary. These words appear in boldface **(dark)** type. Main entries may be single words, compound words, abbreviations, affixes, or phrases.

Compound Words. Compound words may be *open* (written as two words), *hyphenated* (written with a hyphen between the two words), or *closed* (written as one word). All compound words, whether one word or two words, are listed alphabetically, letter by letter, as if they were one word. Check the front matter of the dictionary to see that book's style for showing each type of compound.

Homographs. *Homographs* are words that are spelled alike but have different meanings and origins. They may or may not be pronounced differently. Such words are assigned numbers.

**2.G.2
Main Entries**

vice[1] (evil habit) tear[1] (cry)
vice[2] (a holding tool) tear[2] (rip)
vice[3] (in place of)

Dictionaries show how to pronounce a word by rewriting it with symbols that represent the sounds in the word. A *pronunciation key,* usually at the top or bottom of a page or set of facing pages, helps you translate the symbols for the sounds. Key words for the symbols in the pronunciation key help you determine the sound represented by a symbol.

The pronunciation for a word also shows the syllable divisions for a word. A *syllable* is the part of a word usually pronounced as a unit. An accent mark (') shows which syllable or syllables are said with greater force.

Sometimes multiple pronunciations are given for a word. In this case, the first pronunciation is usually

**2.G.3
Pronunciations**

preferred. However, the first pronunciation may apply when the word is used as a certain part of speech and the second may apply for another part of speech.

re|fund (*v.* ri fund′; *n.* rē′ fund)

2.G.4
Dictionary
Definitions

Good dictionaries include all known definitions of a word. They often include appropriate sentences to illustrate the word's meaning.

2.G.5
Parts of
Speech

Some words can be used as more than one part of speech. A dictionary indicates the parts of speech of words before the appropriate definitions. Abbreviations are used to show the parts of speech. They are not always listed alphabetically. *See also* **4.A**: Parts of Speech.

second:
adj. next after the first: *second* prize.
adv. in the second group: to speak *second.*
n. a person who attends a boxer or a duelist:
The *second* gave the boxer some advice.
vt. to support: I *second* the motion.

2.G.6
Synonym and
Antonym
Studies

A good dictionary helps you learn more about the connotation, that is, the emotional or suggested meaning of synonyms. A synonym study explains the differences among groups of synonyms.

Steal, pilfer, filch mean to take dishonestly. **Steal** is the general and common word: *Thieves tried to steal the crown jewels.* **Pilfer** means to steal and carry away in small amounts: *The number of bolts pilfered from the factory is small.* **Filch** implies stealthy or furtive pilfering of insignificant items: *The boys filched the matches from the mantel.*

Many dictionaries also include antonyms.

Under the entry for *clean,* you might find the antonyms *dirty, filthy, soiled, vile, sordid,* and *squalid.*

2.G.7
Using a
Dictionary
to Spell
Words

Some words have more than one acceptable spelling. Dictionaries list them all. The less acceptable spelling will have a cross reference to the more acceptable spelling of that word.

To find out how to spell a word correctly, first, decide what part of the word you are unsure of. Then look up the word by using the various ways to spell that part of the word.

> To determine whether the word is spelled *seperate* or *separate*, look up *sepa-*.

> <u>See</u> **3.C**: Spelling English Sounds *for possible spellings of many English words.*

The lists on the following pages feature words that you are likely to encounter in various specialized areas such as business, health care, and the law. Determine how many of these words you know well enough to use in your writing and speaking. Then use a dictionary to look up the meanings of words you do not know.

2.H

**Words
Worth
Knowing**

BUSINESS

account	deposit	indemnity	preemption
accredit	depreciate	inflation	premium
affiliate	depression	insolvency	prepayment
agency	disburse	intangible	price
allot	discount	interest	principal amount
amalgamation	diversification	inventory	production
amend	dividend	investment	profit
applicant	double entry	invoice	promissory note
appraisal	down payment	joint account	proprietor
appreciate	draft	layoff	provision
assessment	drawee	lease	realty
assets	duty	legal tender	recession
auditor	economics	lessee	refund
backing	elapse	lessor	remit
balance	embezzle	liquidate	remuneration
bear market	encumbrance	loan	rent
bidding	endorse	lottery	resources
bill of sale	endowment	Ltd.	retail
bond	enterprise	management	retirement
boycott	entrepreneur	margin	return
broker	equity	market	revenue
budget	estate	maximum	risk
bull market	ex-	merchandise	salary
capital	executor	merger	sale
cartel	expenditure	minimum	sell short
census	expiration	minority	shareholder
charter	export	monopoly	simple interest
checkbook	extension	mortgage	speculate
claim	face value	negligence	stock exchange
clause	Federal Reserve	negotiable	sublet
client	Bank	net	supply
COD	finance	notary	surplus
collateral	fiscal year	note	tangible
common stock	FOB	obligation	tariff
compound interest	forecast	organization	technology
consolidation	foreclosure	outgo	tenant
consumption	franchise	outlay	trade
contract	free trade	overdraft	trade union
copyright	fund	ownership	treasurer
corporation	gross	parity	turnover
cost	gross income	partnership	undersigned
credit	guarantor	par value	usury
currency	heir	passbook	utility
dealer	holding	patent	value
decrease	hypothecate	penalty	warranty
deduction	immune	pension	wholesale
default	import	per capita	withdrawal
deficit	incorporate	personnel	write-off

CHEMISTRY

absorption	cellulose	hydrocarbon	properties
acetylene	centrifuge	hydrogen	proton
acid	chlorine	inorganic	radical
agent	chloroform	iodine	radioactive
alcohol	chlorophyll	ion	radium
aldehyde	chromium	iron	radon
alkaline	cobalt	isotope	reactant
alloy	compound	krypton	reagent
alpha ray	concentration	lead	receptacle
alum	condense	liquefy	resin
aluminum	corrosion	litmus	respiration
analyze	cosmetology	lodestone	RNA
antacid	covalence	magnesium	rust
antifreeze	crucible	manganese	saccharin
antihistamine	decomposition	mass	salt
antimatter	dehydration	matter	saturation
antimony	density	mercury	secretion
argon	dextrose	methane	sedative
arsenic	diffusion	methanol	silicon
atom	dilution	mixture	sodium
atomic energy	direct current	molecular weight	solidify
atomic number	dissolve	molecule	soluble
atomic weight	distill	mortar	solution
balanced	DNA	neon	solvent
barbiturate	drug	neutron	specific gravity
barium	ecology	nickel	steroid
base	einsteinium	nicotine	strontium
beta rays	electrolysis	nitric acid	substance
biochemistry	electrolyte	nitrogen	substitution
bismuth	electron	nucleus	sucrose
bond	element	octane	sulfur
boron	enzyme	organic	suspension
bromine	ethylene	osmosis	synthesis
bronze	fermentation	oxidation	synthetic
Bunsen burner	fertilizer	oxygen	tannic acid
burette	filtration	pasteurize	test tube
butane	fluid	periodic table	tin
calcium	formaldehyde	pestle	titanium
californium	formula	petrification	TNT
carbohydrate	gas	phosphorus	toxicology
carbon	germicide	photosynthesis	uranium
carbonation	glucose	pipette	vacuum
carbon dioxide	glycerine	plastic	valence
carbon monoxide	gold	platinum	vapor
carcinogen	gram	plutonium	vinyl
catalyst	helium	potassium	viscosity
caustic	homogenize	precipitate	xenon
cell	hydrates	propane	zinc

GEOGRAPHY

agrarian	distribution	importation	rainfall
agribusiness	district	inhabitant	rain forest
agriculture	divide	inland	range
agronomy	doldrums	inlet	rapids
altitude	domestic	insular	raw material
annual	drainage	international	reef
Antarctic	drought	irrigation	region
Arctic	earth	island	reservoir
area	earthquake	isobar	revolution
arid	east	isotherm	ridge
axis	eclipse	isthmus	rotation
barren	ecology	jungle	rural
basin	equator	latitude	sand bar
bay	erosion	lava	sea level
beach	eruption	levee	seaport
belt	evergreen	location	seismology
blizzard	exportation	lock	settlement
border	extinct	longitude	shoreline
boundary	fallow	lowland	sierra
canal	fertile	mainland	soil
canyon	firth	map	sound
cape	fisheries	meridian	south
cartographer	fjord	migrate	South Pole
channel	flood plain	monsoon	sphere
circumference	forage	mountain chain	steppe
climate	foreign	mouth	strait
climatology	forest	nation	swamp
coast	fossil	natural resources	Temperate Zone
colony	frontier	nomad	temperature
compass	geyser	north	territory
conservation	glacier	North Pole	tornado
consumption	globe	oasis	Torrid Zone
continent	government	oceanography	Tropic of Cancer
continental shelf	grassland	ore	Tropic of Capri-
coral	grid	outlet	corn
country	growing season	peak	tropics
county	gulf	peninsula	tundra
crater	Gulf Stream	petroleum	typhoon
crop	harbor	plain	urban
cultivate	harvest	plateau	valley
current	headland	pogonip	village
cyclone	hemisphere	polar	volcano
dam	highland	population	waterfall
deciduous	hinterland	prairie	watershed
degrees	horizon	precipitation	waterway
delta	humidity	primitive	weather
demography	hurricane	production	west
desert	hybrid	province	westerlies

HEALTH

abscess	corpuscle	intoxication	pneumonia
addiction	cranium	intravenous	polio
adrenalin	cyst	iris	psoriasis
allergy	dehydration	larynx	psychiatric
amnesia	dermatitis	leukemia	psychosis
analgesic	diabetes	ligament	ptomaine
angina	diagnosis	lymph	pyorrhea
antibiotic	diaphragm	malaria	quarantine
antidote	diarrhea	malignant	rabies
antiseptic	diastolic	malnutrition	respiratory
artery	diet	marrow	retina
artificial respira-	dietetic	measles	rheumatism
tion	digitalis	medication	RH factor
aseptic	dilate	membrane	rickets
asthma	diphtheria	meningitis	sanitarium
astigmatism	diuretic	metastasis	sanitation
atrophy	dysentery	migraine	sclerosis
bacteria	dystrophy	minerals	sedative
benign	embryo	molar	septic
botulism	emotion	mononucleosis	serum
bronchitis	emphysema	mucus	shingles
bursitis	enzyme	mumps	sinew
caffeine	epidemic	myelitis	sinusitis
calorie	epidermis	myopia	smallpox
cancer	epileptic	narcotic	spastic
carbohydrate	esophagus	neuralgia	spleen
carcinogen	fibrillation	neuritis	sterile
cardiac	gallstone	neurotic	strep throat
cardiogram	gangrene	nicotine	stress
caries	gastric	nutrient	sulfa
cataract	gene	obese	syndrome
cerebral	germicide	optic	systolic
cervix	glandular	orthodontic	tetanus
chemotherapy	glaucoma	orthopedic	thyroid
cholesterol	halitosis	ovary	tourniquet
chromosome	hepatitis	ovum	toxic
circulatory	hernia	pancreas	trachea
cirrhosis	histamine	pasteurization	tuberculosis
coagulate	hygiene	pelvis	tumor
colon	hypochondria	penicillin	typhoid
coma	immunization	peritonitis	ulcer
communicable	impetigo	phlebitis	umbilical cord
compress	incisor	phobia	uterus
concussion	infectious	pituitary	vaccination
contagious	influenza	placebo	vein
convalesce	inoculation	plaque	venereal
convulsion	insomnia	plasma	vertigo
cornea	insulin	pleurisy	vitamin

HISTORY

abdication	contemporary	franchise	per capita
administration	coronation	freedom	pilgrim
alien	council	free trade	plebeian
amend	coup	frontier	plebiscite
amnesty	creed	government	politician
anarchy	crown	governor	politics
ancestor	crusade	guerrilla	polls
antiquity	culture	hearing	President
apartheid	custom	homeland	primary
appoint	czar	immigrate	prime minister
aristocracy	deflation	imperialism	proletarian
armament	delegate	inauguration	queen
Armistice Day	democracy	industrialization	racial
barbarian	Democrat	inflation	realm
bicameral	depose	internationalism	rebellion
bill	depression	invasion	reign
Bill of Rights	despot	judiciary	representative
blockade	détente	jurisdiction	republic
bourgeois	dictator	king	Republican
bureaucracy	diplomat	labor union	resign
cabinet	disarmament	law	revolution
campaign	dominion	leftist	rightist
capitalism	draft	legislature	right wing
century	duty	levy	rule
charter	dynasty	liberalism	secede
circumnavigate	economy	loyalist	secretary
citizen	election	Magna Carta	serf
civil	electoral college	majority	settler
civilization	electorate	Mayflower	slavery
Civil War	Emancipation	medieval	socialism
coalition	Proclamation	military	society
coexistence	embargo	minority	statecraft
Cold War	emigrate	minuteman	states' rights
colonist	emperor	monarch	strategy
commerce	empire	monopoly	Supreme Court
communism	enlist	nationalism	taxation
Confederacy	enslave	nationalization	Tory
Congress	era	neutrality	totalitarian
congressional	establishment	nobility	tradition
conquer	executive	office	treason
conscription	exploration	official	tribe
conservatism	fascism	oligarchy	truce
conservative	federal	pacifist	unicameral
constituency	federation	parliamentary	United States
constitution	feminist	party	USSR
constitutional	feudalism	patrician	vice-president
consul	foreign policy	Pentagon	vote

LANGUAGE

abbreviation
ablative
abstract
accusative
active
adjective
adverb
affix
agreement
allegory
alliteration
allusion
antecedent
antonym
apostrophe
appositive
archaism
augmentative
auxiliary
bibliography
biography
blank verse
case
clause
cliché
coherence
collective noun
colloquial
colon
comedy
common noun
comparative
   degree
complement
complex sentence
compound
   sentence
conjunction
connotation
contraction
correlative
declarative
demonstrative
   pronoun
denotation
dependent clause
derivation
diacritical mark

diagram
dialect
diction
diminutive
direct object
double negative
drama
elegy
elliptical clause
emphasis
epic
epigram
eponym
essay
etymology
euphemism
euphony
exclamatory
exposition
fable
feminine
fiction
figure of speech
free verse
future
gender
genitive
gerund
glossary
grammar
homily
homonym
hyperbole
hyphen
iambic
idiomatic
imperative
independent
   clause
index
indicative
indirect object
infinitive
inflection
intensive
interjection
interrogative
intonation

intransitive
irony
jargon
linking verb
literature
litotes
lyric
main clause
masculine
metaphor
meter
metonymy
modify
mood
narration
neologism
neuter
nominative
nonfiction
noun
number
ode
onomatopoeia
oxymoron
parable
paragraph
paraphrase
parody
participle
passive
pejorative
pentameter
perfect
phrase
pitch
plagiarism
plot
plural
poetry
positive degree
possessive
predicate
preface
prefix
preposition
pronoun
pronunciation
proper noun

prose
proverb
pun
punctuation
quotation
redundancy
referent
reflexive
rhyme
rhythm
root word
run-on sentence
sarcasm
satire
semantics
semicolon
sentence
short story
simile
slang
soliloquy
sonnet
split infinitive
stanza
subject
subjunctive
subordinate
   clause
suffix
superlative degree
syllabification
synecdoche
synonym
synopsis
syntax
tense
thesaurus
topic sentence
tragedy
transitive
trite
trochaic
unity
usage
verb
vernacular
verse
vocabulary

LAW

abduction	counterfeit	judgment	plea bargaining
accessory	court	judicial	police
accomplice	court-martial	juror	prison
accuse	crime	jury	probation
acquit	criminal	justice	prosecutor
adult	damages	juvenile court	public defender
affidavit	decision	kidnap	quorum
alias	deed	kleptomania	ransom
alimony	defendant	larceny	rape
amend	defense	law	repeal
amendment	delinquent	lawful	resist
annul	deposition	lawsuit	right
appeal	detention	lawyer	robbery
apprehension	district attorney	legal	ruling
arbitration	divorce	legitimate	search warrant
arrest	embezzle	libel	self-defense
arson	enact	license	sentence
assassination	enforcement	lie detector	sheriff
assault	eviction	line-up	slander
assault and	evidence	magistrate	smuggle
battery	execution	malice	solitary confine-
attorney	eyewitness	malpractice	ment
autopsy	felony	manslaughter	sue
bail	fine	martial law	suit
ban	fingerprint	minor	summons
bankruptcy	forgery	Miranda card	Supreme Court
battery	frame	misdemeanor	suspect
bench	grand jury	mistrial	swear
bigamy	grand larceny	murder	swear in
birthright	guilt	negligence	tax dodging
blackmail	habeas corpus	negotiate	testify
break-in	hearing	nonsupport	testimony
bribery	heir	notary public	theft
burglary	hijack	null and void	treason
capital punish-	homicide	oath	trespass
ment	hung jury	offense	trial
case	immunity	officer	trust
citizenship	impeach	pardon	try
civil liberties	imprison	parole	unconstitutional
civil rights	incompetent	patent	vandalism
commute	indict	patrol	verdict
confession	informer	penal	violate
conspiracy	innocent	perjury	warden
constitution	inquiry	petition	warrant
contract	interrogation	petty larceny	will
convict	jail	plaintiff	wiretapping
counselor	judge	plea	witness

MATHEMATICS

abscissa	deviation	invariable	product
absolute	diagonal	inverse	proportion
acute	diagram	invert	pyramid
addition	diameter	isosceles	quadrangle
adjacent	difference	kilometer	quadratic
algebra	digit	length	quantities
analysis	dimension	line	quotient
angle	direction	linear	radian
apex	distance	logarithm	radical
arabic numerals	distribution	logic	radius
arc	divide	mathematics	range
area	dividend	maximum	rate
arithmetic	divisor	mean	ratio
array	double	measure	real numbers
average	dozen	median	reciprocal
axiom	eliminate	meter	rectangle
axis	ellipse	mile	remainder
base	empty set	minimum	right angle
binomial	equal	minus	roman numerals
bisect	equal sets	multiple	root
calculation	equation	multiply	rotation
calculus	equilateral	negative	round off
cancellation	equivalent	nonagon	segment
Celsius tempera-	even numbers	number	semicircle
ture	exponent	numeral	set
centimeter	extract	numerator	simplify
circle	face value	obtuse	slide rule
circumference	factor	octagon	solid
component	Fahrenheit	odd numbers	solution
composite	figure	operation	space
computation	finite	ordinate	sphere
computer	focus	origin	square
congruent	formula	ounce	square root
conversion	fraction	parabola	statistics
convex	frequency	parallel	subtract
cube	function	pentagon	sum
curve	geometry	per cent	symbol
data	heptagon	perimeter	symmetry
decagon	hexagon	perpendicular	system
decibel	hypotenuse	pi	tangent
decimal	hypothesis	plane	term
deduction	inch	plus	tetrahedron
deficit	increase	point	theorem
degree	inequality	polygon	trapezoid
denominator	infinite	positive	triangle
denotation	integer	pound	trigonometry
depth	intersect	power	volume
derivation	interval	probability	width

PHYSICAL SCIENCE

absolute zero
acoustics
aerodynamics
aerosol
aerospace
alloy
alternator
ampere
amplifier
anemometer
anode
armature
asteroid
atom
ballast
barometer
battery
calibrate
calipers
cam
catalytic converter
cathode
centigrade
centrifugal
centripetal
chain reaction
charge
circuit
compound
concave
conductor
convert
convex
cosmic ray
current
data
decibel
declination
deduce
dehumidifier
dehydrate
differential
diffraction
dimension
direct current
discharge
distillation
dry cell

dynamo
E = mc²
electric
electrode
electromagnet
electron
element
energy
equilibrium
erg
Fahrenheit
fission
fulcrum
fusion
generator
gram
gravity
humidistat
hydraulic
hydroelectric
hydrometer
incandescent
inertia
infrared
insulation
intensity
internal combus-
    tion
ion
ionosphere
isotope
kilogram
kilowatt
laboratory
laser
launch
lens
lever
light-year
linear
magnetic field
magnify
maser
matrix
matter
mechanics
megahertz
megaton

meteorology
metric
microfilm
microscope
microwave
modulation
molten
momentum
motion
motor
negative
neutron
nova
nuclear
nucleus
odometer
orbit
ore
oxidation
ozone
parameter
penumbra
photoelectric
photon
physics
physiology
plastic
pole
polygon
positive
power pack
pressure
prism
propellant
proton
pulsar
quasar
radar
radiation
radioactive
radiometer
radiotelescope
ray
reflect
refract
relativity
resistor
retrorocket

rotation
seismograph
short circuit
simulation
smelter
solar
solar cell
sonar
sonic boom
sound barrier
specific gravity
spectrum
stabilizer
static
static electricity
stress
subsonic
substance
sunspot
supersonic
symmetrical
tachometer
tension
terminal
thermal
thermodynamics
thermonuclear
thermostat
thrust
torque
transformer
transistor
transmission
transmute
turbine
ultrasonic
ultraviolet
uranium
vacuum
vector
vertex
volt
volume
watt
wavelength
weight density
wet cell
worm gear

RELIGION

abbey	cult	Jesus	reincarnation
absolution	damnation	Jew	religion
Advent	devil	Koran	repent
agnostic	devout	laity	resurrect
Allah	disciple	Lent	revelation
almighty	divine	Lord	rite
altar	dogma	Lutheran	rosary
amen	Easter	Madonna	Sabbath
angel	ecumenical	Magi	sacrament
apostle	ethics	martyr	sacred
archangel	Eucharist	mass	sacrilege
atheist	evangelism	Messiah	sacristy
atonement	evil	Methodist	saint
baptism	exalt	minister	salvation
Baptist	excommunicate	miracle	sanctify
bar mitzvah	Exodus	missionary	Satan
bas mitzvah	faith	Mohammed	Savior
beatitude	feast	monastery	scripture
Bible	forgiveness	monk	seminary
bishop	free will	mortal	sermon
blaspheme	fundamentalist	nave	Shinto
blessing	genesis	nun	sin
breviary	gentile	offertory	soul
Buddhism	genuflect	ordain	spiritual
canonize	God	orthodox	Star of David
canticle	golden rule	papacy	synagogue
cantor	gospel	parable	tabernacle
cardinal	grace	parochial	Taoism
Catholic	Grail	pastor	temple
celibacy	hallow	penance	Ten Command-
chalice	Hanukkah	Pentecost	ments
chapel	heaven	pilgrimage	Tenebrae
choir	Hebrew	pious	Testament
Christ	Hegira	Pope	theology
christen	hell	pray	tithe
Christian	heresy	preach	Torah
church	heterodoxy	Presbyterian	transept
clergy	high priest	priest	trespass
commandment	holy	prophet	Trinity
communion	Holy Ghost	Protestant	Vatican
confession	hope	psalm	verse
confirmation	idol	pulpit	vespers
Confucius	Immaculate	purgatory	vestibule
congregation	Conception	purification	Virgin Mary
convent	immortal	Puritan	worship
creed	incarnation	Quaker	Yom Kippur
cross	Islam	rabbi	zealot
crucifix	Jehovah	redemption	Zionism

Chapter

3

Spelling

Spelling words correctly is an important part of writing. By following guidelines for improving spelling, becoming aware of common mispronunciations, and knowing which letters or group of letters spell English sounds, you can become a more effective speller. Learning spelling rules that apply to a large percentage of English words, knowing the difference between spellings of homophones, as well as mastering frequently misspelled words also can increase your spelling ability.

 NOTE: For additional help with spelling, *see* **2.G.7**: Using a Dictionary to Spell Words.

3.A

Guidelines for Improving Spelling

Each of the following suggestions will help you become a more effective speller.

1. Consult a dictionary or word list handbook whenever you are in doubt about the correct spelling of a word.

2. Use memory aids to learn word spellings. These might be jingles, rhymes, word games, or word associations. Even silly, far-fetched methods, such as the following, may help you.

    There is *a rat* in *separate*.
    A *laboratory* is a place where people *labor*.

3. Keep an individual word list of all the words you misspell.

4. Proofread all written materials.

NOTE: It is important to read over all materials even if you use a spell-checking system on a computer. Spell-checking systems cannot detect incorrect homophone use or words misspelled in such a way that they spell another word.

5. Use your senses to learn to spell a word.

See the word's beginning and ending letters, then the word as a whole. Next, close your eyes and try to remember how it looks.

Say the word, being sure to pronounce it correctly. Divide the word into syllables and say them distinctly. Then spell the word aloud.

Write the word a number of times until you can do it without really thinking about it.

6. Use the word when speaking and writing. Make up a sentence using it with its most common meaning.

A person who mispronounces a word by rearranging, adding, or deleting sounds will very likely spell that word incorrectly. *See* **14.A.3**: Articulation and Pronunciation Problems *and* **2.G.3**: Pronunciations. The list below shows some words that are often mispronounced and, as a result, misspelled.

3.B

Mispronunciation

antarctic, not antartic
athlete, not athalete
barbarous, not barbarious
burglar, not burgaler
candidate, not canidate
congratulate, not congradulate
divide, not devide
divine, not devine
drowned, not drownded
escape, not excape
evidently, not evadently
February, not Febuary
government, not goverment
hungry, not hungery
jewelry, not jewlry
kindergarten, not kindygarten

library, not libary
mischievous, not mischievious
nuclear, not nucular
perform, not preform
perspire, not prespire
poem, not pome
practically, not practicly
probably, not probly
quantity, not quanity
similar, not similiar
sophomore, not sophmore
studying, not studing
surprise, not suprise
temperament, not temprament
temperature, not temprature

3.C

Spelling English Sounds

Many English sounds can be spelled several different ways.

bene*fit*   *ph*rase   enou*gh*

Each word contains a letter or group of letters that represents the *f* sound, but the spelling of the sound is different in each case.

Although there are no rules to tell you how a given sound will always be spelled in any particular case, it is still helpful to know the possible ways a sound *may* be spelled. The following table shows some possible spellings for many English sounds.

Spellings of English Sounds

THE SOUND	AS IN	MAY BE SPELLED	AS IN
short *a*	hat	*ai*	pl*ai*d
		au	l*au*gh
long *a*	ape	*ai*	*ai*d
		ay	pl*ay*
		ea	br*ea*k
		ei	*ei*ght
		ey	th*ey*
short *e*	set	*a*	m*a*ny
		ai	s*ai*d
		ay	s*ay*s
long *e*	she	*ae*	C*ae*sar
		i	mach*i*ne
		ie	bel*ie*ve
short *i*	h*i*m	*ee*	b*ee*n
		o	w*o*men
		u	b*u*sy
		y	h*y*mn
long *i*	ice	*ai*	*ai*sle
		ei	h*ei*ght
		y	st*y*le
short *o*	lot	*a*	w*a*tt
long *o*	open	*ew*	s*ew*
		oa	m*oa*t
		oe	h*oe*
		oo	br*oo*ch
		ou	s*ou*l
		ow	sl*ow*

THE SOUND	AS IN	MAY BE SPELLED	AS IN
short *u*	c*u*p	*o*	c*o*me
		ou	d*ou*ble
y*ü*	*yu*le	*eu*	f*eu*d
		ew	f*ew*
		u	*u*se
		ue	c*ue*
f	*f*un	*gh*	enou*gh*
		ph	*ph*oto
g	*g*o	*gh*	*gh*ost
		gue	ro*gue*
j	*j*ar	*dg*	ri*dg*e
		g	fra*g*ile
m	*m*e	*lm*	ca*lm*
		mb	cli*mb*
n	*n*o	*gn*	*gn*at
		kn	*kn*ow
		pn	*pn*eumonia
ng	thi*ng*	*n*	thi*n*k
r	*r*un	*rh*	*rh*yme
		wr	*wr*ong
s	*s*ay	*c*	*c*ent
		ce	ri*ce*
		ps	*ps*ychology
sh	*sh*e	*ch*	ma*ch*ine
		ci	spe*ci*al
		ti	na*ti*on
t	*t*ell	*ed*	dropp*ed*
z	*z*oo	*s*	de*s*ert
		sc	di*sc*ern
		ss	de*ss*ert
		x	*x*ylophone

Spelling rules can help answer many of your spelling questions. Become as familiar as possible with the following rules. Then refer back to the table whenever you have a specific question or wish to refresh your memory.

NOTE: Remember that there are exceptions to almost every spelling rule. Be sure to pay as much attention to the exceptions as to the rules.

3.D

Spelling Rules

Table of Spelling Rules

PROBLEMS	RULE	SOME EXCEPTIONS
Words with *i*'s and *e*'s: *believe, deceit*	Use *i* before *e* except after *c* or when sounded like *a* as in *neighbor* and *weigh*.	*ancient, financier, counterfeit, either, foreign, height, leisure, seize, weird*
Words ending in *cede: precede*	The root *cede* is always spelled this way except in four words and their various forms.	*supersede, exceed, proceed, succeed* and their other forms *(superseded, exceeding, proceeds, succeeder)*
Words ending in *c: traffic*	Insert *k* when adding an ending that begins with *e, i,* or *y: trafficked.*	*arced*
Words ending in soft *ce* or *ge: peace, advantage*	Retain the final *e* before adding *able* or *ous: peaceable, advantageous.*	
Words ending in silent *e: desire*	Drop the final *e* before suffixes beginning with a vowel: *desirable.*	*mileage*
Words ending in silent *e: love*	Retain the final *e* before suffixes beginning with a consonant: *lovely.*	*acknowledgment, argument, duly, judgment, ninth, wholly*
Words ending in *ie: tie*	Change *ie* to *y* when adding *ing: tying.*	
Words ending in *oe: hoe*	Retain the final *e* before a suffix beginning with any vowel except *e: hoeing* but *hoed.*	
Words ending in *y* preceded by a consonant: *occupy*	Change *y* to *i* before a suffix unless the suffix begins with *i: occupies* but *occupying.*	
Adjectives of one syllable ending in *y: dry*	Retain *y* when adding a suffix: *drying.*	
Words of one syllable and words accented on the last syllable, ending in a consonant preceded by a vowel: *glad, repel, occur*	Double the consonant before a suffix beginning with a vowel: *gladden, repelled, occurred.*	*crocheting, ricocheted, filleted, transferable* (but *transferred*) Also, if the accent shifts to the first syllable when a suffix is added, the final consonant is not doubled: *preferred,* but *preference.*

PROBLEMS	RULE	SOME EXCEPTIONS
Words ending in a consonant preceded by more than one vowel: *boil, reveal*	Do not double the consonant before a suffix beginning with a vowel: *boiled, revealing.*	
Words ending in more than one consonant: *work, conform*	Do not double the final consonant: *worked, conforming.*	
Words not accented on the last syllable: *benefit*	Do not double the final consonant: *benefited.*	
Words ending in *l*: *horizontal*	Retain the *l* before a suffix beginning with *l*: *horizontally.*	Words ending in *ll* drop one *l* before the suffix *ly*: *hilly, fully.*
Prefixes and suffixes ending in *ll*: *all-, -full*	Omit one *l* when adding these to other words: *almost, grateful.*	
Prefixes *dis-, il-, im-, in-, mis-, over-, re-, un-*	Do not change the spelling of the root word: *dissimilar, illegal, immoral, innumerable, misspell, overrun, reedit, unnerve.*	
Words ending in a double consonant: *possess, enroll*	Retain both consonants when adding suffixes: *possessor, enrolling.*	
Nouns ending in *f* or *fe*: *handkerchief*	Form the plural by adding *s*: *handkerchiefs.*	Some nouns ending in *f* or *fe* form the plural by changing the *f* or *fe* to *ve* and adding *s*: *knives, elves, halves, leaves, loaves, shelves, wives.*
Nouns ending in *y* preceded by a consonant: *lady*	Form the plural by changing *y* to *i* and adding *es*: *ladies.*	Proper nouns ending in *y* form the plural by adding *s*: "Three *Garys* work in my office."
Nouns ending in *ch, sh, s, x, z*: *gas, church, brush, glass, fox, topaz*	Form the plural by adding *es*: *gases, churches, brushes, glasses, foxes, topazes.*	
Nouns ending in *o* preceded by a vowel: *cameo*	Form the plural by adding *s*: *cameos.*	

PROBLEMS	RULE	SOME EXCEPTIONS
Nouns ending in *o* preceded by a consonant: *potato*	Form the plural by adding *es: potatoes.*	*dittos, dynamos, silos* For some nouns, either *s* or *es* is correct; *buffalos* or *buffaloes, volcanos* or *volcanoes.*
Compound nouns: *major general, notary public, sister-in-law*	Make the modified word plural: major *generals, notaries* public, *sisters*-in-law.	
Nouns ending in *ful: cupful*	Form the plural by adding *s* to *ful: cupfuls.*	
Letters, numbers, dates, signs, and words referred to as words	Form the plural by adding *'s:* six *b's,* two *5's,* the *1970's, %'s, but's.*	

3.E

Homo-phones

Many misspelled words are *homophones*—words that have the same pronunciation but different meanings and different spellings. Writers must know which spelling is correct for their intended meaning.

The list below shows some of the most common homophones. If there are any words you do not understand, look them up in a dictionary. *See* 2.G: Using a Dictionary.

HOMOPHONE LIST			
aid	ant	bad	bate
aide	aunt	bade	bait
air	arc	bail	bazaar
heir	ark	bale	bizarre
ere	assent	ball	be
e'er	ascent	bawl	bee
ale	ate	band	bear
ail	eight	banned	bare
all	auger	bard	beet
awl	augur	barred	beat
aloud	aught	baron	bell
allowed	ought	barren	belle
altar	aye	bass	berth
alter	eye	base	birth

HOMOPHONE LIST

bier	brows	clause	dun
beer	browse	claws	done
bin	burro	click	dying
been	burrow	clique	dyeing
block	borough	clime	earn
bloc	bury	climb	urn
blue	berry	close	ewe
blew	but	clothes	yew
bole	butt	colonel	you
boll	by	kernel	eyelet
bowl	buy	core	islet
bore	bye	corps	faint
boar	calendar	corespondent	feint
bored	calender	correspondent	fair
board	callous	council	fare
born	callus	counsel	faker
borne	cannon	course	fakir
bouillon	canon	coarse	fate
bullion	canvas	coward	fete
bow	canvass	cowered	faun
beau	capital	creek	fawn
bow	capitol	creak	faze
bough	carrot	crews	phase
bowled	carat	cruise	feet
bold	caret	cruse	feat
boy	karat	cue	feign
buoy	cask	queue	fain
brake	casque	current	ferule
break	cast	currant	ferrule
braze	caste	dam	find
braise	ceiling	damn	fined
breach	sealing	dear	fir
breech	cellar	deer	fur
bred	seller	dew	flair
bread	chews	due	flare
brews	choose	die	flee
bruise	choir	dye	flea
bridal	quire	discreet	flew
bridle	choral	discrete	flue
broach	coral	doe	flu
brooch	chord	dough	flour
	cord		flower

HOMOPHONE LIST

fold	heart	least	maze
foaled	hart	leased	maize
fore	heel	led	mead
four	heal	lead	mede
foreward	he'll	lee	medal
forward	herd	lea	meddle
foul	heard	lei	meet
fowl	here	lay	meat
fourth	hear	lesson	mete
forth	him	lessen	metal
frieze	hymn	liar	mettle
frees	hoard	lyre	mien
freeze	horde	liken	mean
gamble	hoarse	lichen	might
gambol	horse	lo	mite
gate	hoes	low	mind
gait	hose	load	mined
gauge	holy	lode	minor
gage	wholly	lone	miner
gild	holey	loan	moan
guild	hour	loot	mown
gilt	our	lute	moat
guilt	hue	lye	mote
gnu	hew	lie	morn
knew	idle	maid	mourn
new	idol	made	muse
great	I'll	male	mews
grate	isle	mail	mussel
grisly	aisle	mane	muscle
grizzly	indict	main	mustered
grown	indite	manner	mustard
groan	jam	manor	nave
guessed	jamb	mantel	knave
guest	knows	mantle	naval
hail	nose	marry	navel
hale	lane	merry	nay
hangar	lain	marshal	neigh
hanger	leaf	martial	need
hare	lief	maul	knead
hair	leak	mall	kneed
haul	leek	maybe	night
hall	lean	may be	knight
	lien		

HOMOPHONE LIST

no	peer	read	sale
know	pier	reed	sail
noes	piece	real	seam
nose	peace	reel	seem
knows	plane	reck	sear
none	plain	wreck	seer
nun	plate	red	sere
not	plait	read	see
knot	please	rest	sea
oar	pleas	wrest	seed
ore	plum	right	cede
o'er	plumb	write	seen
ode	pole	rite	scene
owed	poll	wright	sees
one	pore	rime	seize
won	pour	rhyme	sell
oral	praise	ring	cell
aural	prays	wring	sense
pair	preys	rock	cense
pear	pray	roc	cents
pare	prey	rode	sent
palate	principal	road	cent
pallet	principle	rowed	scent
palette	quartz	roe	serial
pale	quarts	row	cereal
pail	rabbit	roll	session
pane	rabbet	role	cession
pain	rack	root	shear
passed	wrack	route	sheer
past	racket	rows	shoe
patients	racquet	rose	shoo
patience	rain	rude	shone
paws	rein	rood	shown
pause	reign	ruff	sight
peak	raise	rough	site
peek	raze	rung	cite
pique	rays	wrung	sign
pearl	rap	rye	sine
purl	wrap	wry	skull
peddle	rapt	sac	scull
pedal	rapped	sack	slay
peel	wrapped		sleigh
peal			

HOMOPHONE LIST

slight	stoup	the	vein
sleight	stoop	thee	vain
sloe	strait	there	vane
slow	straight	their	vial
so	style	they're	vile
sow	stile	threw	vice
sew	succor	through	vise
soar	sucker	throne	wade
sore	suite	thrown	weighed
soared	sweet	throws	wait
sword	sunny	throes	weight
sold	sonny	tic	waste
soled	surf	tick	waist
some	serf	timber	wave
sum	surge	timbre	waive
son	serge	time	way
sun	tale	thyme	weigh
soul	tail	toe	we
sole	taught	tow	wee
staid	taut	told	wear
stayed	tax	tolled	ware
stare	tacks	two	week
stair	tea	to	weak
stationery	tee	too	whole
stationary	team	use	hole
steak	teem	yews	who's
stake	tear	ewes	whose
steal	tare	vale	wood
steel	tear	veil	would
step	tier		wreak
steppe			reek

3.F

Commonly Misspelled Words

Some English words are commonly misspelled either because the rules for their spellings are difficult to remember or because their spellings do not follow any particular rules. *See also* exceptions listed in the Table of Spelling Rules in **3.D**: Spelling Rules.

The following list presents words that are commonly misspelled.

NOTE: If you are keeping a list of words that cause you spelling problems, you may want to add some of the words from this list. Then use the methods described earlier for learning to spell them. *See* **3.A**: Guidelines for Improving Spelling.

COMMONLY MISSPELLED WORDS

absence	awkward	correspondent	expense
acceptance	bachelor	counterfeit	experience
accessible	because	courageous	extraordinary
accidentally	beggar	courteous	facsimile
accommodate	bicycle	dealt	familiar
accomplish	boundary	debt	fascinating
ache	bulletin	deceased	fasten
achievement	bureau	definite	fiery
acquaintance	business	description	forehead
acquire	cafeteria	desperate	forfeit
acquitted	cancellation	despise	forty
across	captain	develop	freight
advantageous	carburetor	dilemma	friend
advice	career	disappear	fulfill
advisable	ceiling	disastrous	fundamental
affidavit	cemetery	discipline	gauge
aggravate	census	discrepancy	genius
aghast	changeable	disease	governor
allege	characteristic	doctor	grammar
allotment	chauffeur	ecclesiastical	guarantee
all right	chocolate	ecstasy	guerrilla
ally	collateral	efficient	guess
already	colonel	eighth	gypsy
amateur	column	elementary	handsome
analysis	coming	eligible	hangar
anesthetic	commercial	embarrass	happening
angel	commission	eminent	harass
angle	committee	emphasize	height
annual	community	encumbrances	heinous
answer	compel	enforceable	history
anxiety	conceivable	envelope	huge
apparent	condemn	environment	hygiene
appetite	confidence	exaggerate	hypocrisy
appropriate	conscience	excellent	illiterate
approximately	control	exercise	imitate
ascend	controversial	exhilarating	immediately
ascertain	convenience	exhort	impossible
assistant	convertible	existence	incidentally
auxiliary	copyright	expedition	independent

COMMONLY MISSPELLED WORDS

indictment	noticeable	questionnaire	statistics
indispensable	obstacle	quiet	strength
inevitable	occasionally	quite	strictly
innocent	occurrence	raise	susceptible
inoculate	often	realize	sugar
interfere	omitted	receipt	superintendent
iridescent	operate	receive	surgeon
irrelevant	optimistic	recognize	sympathetic
itinerary	ordinarily	referred	synonym
knowledge	origin	reign	temporary
laboratory	original	relevant	therefore
legitimate	outrageous	rendezvous	thorough
liaison	pageant	repeat	tomorrow
license	paralleled	rescind	tragedy
lieutenant	parliament	reservoir	tranquillity
lightning	pastime	resistance	truly
likely	peculiar	resource	twelfth
liquefy	permanent	restaurant	typical
literature	perseverance	rheumatism	until
livelihood	personnel	rhythm	vacillate
magnificent	phenomenal	ridiculous	vacuum
maintenance	Philippines	roommate	vague
maneuver	philosophy	sacrifice	variety
marriage	picnicking	sacrilegious	vegetable
mathematics	pleasant	scarcely	vengeance
medicine	politician	schedule	vilify
millionaire	Portuguese	scissors	villain
miniature	possession	scurrilous	warrant
minuscule	possibility	secretary	wear
minute	prairie	semester	Wednesday
miscellaneous	prejudiced	sentence	whether
mischief	preparation	separate	won't
mortgage	pretension	sergeant	would
muscle	privilege	shepherd	writer
mystery	procedure	siege	writing
necessary	proceedings	significance	written
nickel	professor	skein	wrote
niece	proffered	skiing	yacht
night	promissory	skillful	yield
ninety	pronunciation	souvenir	
noisily	pursue	specimen	

Grammar

Using proper grammar is an essential part of communicating clearly and effectively. Learning the eight parts of speech, the parts of a sentence, and the different kinds of sentences will help you master the rules of grammar. *See also* **1.B.3**: Grammar and Usage Evolution.

Every word in a sentence has a function. When you identify exactly what a word does in a sentence, the word can be classified as a particular *part of speech*. Traditional grammars list eight parts of speech: nouns, pronouns, adjectives, verbs, adverbs, prepositions, conjunctions, and interjections.

4.A
Parts of Speech

Some words act only as one part of speech. Others may act as several, depending on how the word is used. For example, the word *down* may function as a noun, a preposition, or an adverb.

The quarterback passed on third *down*.
(noun)

The ball sailed *down* the field.
(preposition)

The receiver fell *down*.
(adverb)

When you read, write, or speak, you probably do not bother to classify words as particular parts of speech. There is no reason for you to do so most of the time. But when you want to identify and correct grammatical errors, it is very helpful to understand what the parts of speech are and how they function. The next part of this chapter explains the eight parts of speech and shows how to use them correctly.

4.A.1
Nouns

A *noun* is a word that names a person, place, thing, idea, action, or quality.

4.A.1.a
Common and Proper Nouns

There are two kinds of nouns: proper and common. *Proper nouns* name particular persons, places, or things.

> Susan   Gray Road

It is easy to recognize these nouns because they are written with capital letters.

Common nouns name a type of person, place, or thing.

> man   store   lamp

Common nouns may be further divided into three groups: abstract, concrete, and collective.

Abstract Nouns. *Abstract nouns* name intangibles—things that cannot be seen or touched—such as qualities, actions, and ideas.

> courage   helpfulness   loyalty

Most of the time, you use *the* before abstract nouns rather than *a* or *an*.

Concrete Nouns. *Concrete nouns* name things that you can see or touch.

> door   pencil   car

You may find either *a, an,* or *the* before concrete nouns, depending on the meaning you wish to convey.

Collective Nouns. *Collective nouns* name groups of people or things.

> audience   herd   set

When a collective noun refers to a group as a unit, any verbs and pronouns related to the noun are singular. *See also* 5.B.1.a: Subject-Verb Agreement.

> The *audience is* enjoying the symphony.
> The *herd heads* toward *its* new pasture.

When a collective noun refers to the individual members of the group, any verbs and pronouns related to the noun are plural.

The *panel* submitted *their* opinions.
The *gang are* all going *their* separate ways.

NOTE: In the past, many universally used nouns were exclusively masculine in gender. Although they were used to apply to both sexes, they appeared to exclude women. More recently, nonsexist language has evolved which, in more inclusive neutral terms, applies to both sexes. Careful writers and speakers try to use nonsexist terms which apply to *people* in general. The following list presents some modern alternatives for masculine nouns and terms. For a similar consideration with pronouns, see also the note at the end of **4.A.2.g**: Agreement of Pronouns.

Instead of:	Use:
businessmen	business leaders, merchants, industrialists
brotherhood	unity, community
cameramen	photographers, camera operators
cavemen	early people, primitive people, prehistoric people
chairman	chairperson, chair, moderator, department head
craftsmen	craftworkers, artisans
deliverymen	delivery persons, delivery drivers
draftsmen	drafters
firemen	fire fighters
forefathers	ancestors
foremen	supervisors
lumbermen	loggers
mailmen	mail carriers, postal workers
makeup men	makeup artists
mankind	humankind, humanity
manpower	work force, personnel, workers
men	humans, human beings, people, persons
policemen	police officers
salesmen	salespersons, salesclerks
showmen	performers
sound men	sound technicians
spokesmen	spokespersons, representatives
workmen	workers

NOTE *(continued):* Terms such as the following on the left are no longer generally accepted. Use those on the right instead.

Instead of:	Use:
ambassadress	ambassador
authoress	author
aviatrix	aviator
coed	student
housewife	homemaker
poetess	poet
sculptress	sculptor
stewardess/steward	flight attendant

**4.A.1.b
Singular and
Plural Nouns**

A noun is *singular* if it names one person or thing.

> child   rock   mouse

A noun is *plural* if it names more than one person or thing.

> children   rocks   mice

Most nouns change their form when they are expressed in the plural.

> cat—cats   church—churches

You can form most plurals by simply adding *-s* or *-es*. The spelling of some nouns changes more markedly to form the plural.

> child—children   woman—women   mouse—mice
> shelf—shelves   foot—feet

The spelling of some nouns does not change at all in the plural.

> one sheep—two sheep   one deer—two deer

Consult a dictionary whenever you are in doubt about the correct way to form the plural of a noun. *See* **2.G**: Using a Dictionary. *See also* **5.B.1.a**: Subject-Verb Agreement.

**4.A.1.c
Appositives**

An *appositive* is a noun, or a group of words acting as a noun, that means the same thing, explains, or elaborates on the preceding noun.

> *Carol,* my best *friend,* is moving to Toledo.
> (friend = Carol)

Lou's *neighbor, Chuck Matts,* won a seat on the city council.
(Chuck Matts = neighbor)

Harry's long-standing *dream, to visit California*, finally came true.
(to visit California = dream)

I enjoy playing two *sports, football* and *soccer.*
(football, soccer = sports)

Nouns change their form to show possession.

Aristotle's philosophy   the painter's studio
the scouts' leader

All singular nouns form the possessive by adding an apostrophe and -*s.*

Churchill's speeches   the President's policies

NOTE: Singular nouns that end in -*s* may form the possessive by adding an apostrophe and -*s* or an apostrophe only. However, just adding an apostrophe is more common.

Charles' desk   Charles's desk

Plural nouns that end in -*s* form the possessive by adding an apostrophe only.

soldiers' orders   mayors' proclamations

Plural nouns that do not end in -*s* form the possessive by adding an apostrophe and -*s.*

people's opinions   children's clothing

In cases of joint possession, only the last word shows possession.

Jack and Barbara's dog
Mother and Father's car

When two or more persons possess something individually, both words show possession.

Helen's and Linda's books
Dorothy Johnson's and David Washington's law firms

In compound nouns (nouns made of more than one word) only the last word shows possession.

father-in-law's   editor-in-chief's

4.A.2
Pronouns

A *pronoun* is a word that takes the place of a noun. Pronouns stand for people or things without naming them.

There are five kinds of pronouns: personal, relative, demonstrative, indefinite, and interrogative.

4.A.2.a
Personal
Pronouns

Personal pronouns indicate by their form whether the pronoun refers to the person speaking (first person), the person spoken to (second person), or the person or thing spoken about (third person).

First person

Singular: I; my, mine; me   *Plural*: we; our, ours; us

Second person

Singular: you; your, yours; you   *Plural*: you; your, yours; you

Third person

Singular:
Masculine: he; his; him
Feminine: she; her, hers; her
Neuter: it; its; it

Plural:
they; their, theirs; them

Reflexive pronouns are formed by adding *-self* or *-selves* to the personal pronouns.

myself   yourself   herself   himself   itself
ourselves yourselves   themselves

These pronouns are called reflexive because they indicate that the action of the verb is turned back on the subject.

My baby brother just learned how to feed *himself*.

Reflexive pronouns are intensive when they give emphasis to the subject.

I *myself* made that table.

NOTE: A reflexive pronoun cannot be used alone. It must refer to someone.

Incorrect: They asked *myself and Sue* to join them.
Correct: *Todd* looked at *himself* in the mirror.

For a discussion of the different forms that personal pronouns take, *see* **4.A.2.f**: Case of Pronouns.

Relative pronouns introduce adjective clauses. *See* **4.B.4.b**: Dependent Clauses. The relative pronouns are *who, whose, whom, which,* and *that.*

**4.A.2.b
Relative
Pronouns**

> Mr. Samuels is the architect *who* designed our new library.
>
> The mystery book, *which* was a gift from Claire's brother, held her spellbound from beginning to end.
>
> The committee *that* formulated this plan has been commended.

Demonstrative pronouns are used to point out or designate particular people, places, or things. The demonstrative pronouns are *this, that, these,* and *those.*

**4.A.2.c
Demonstrative
Pronouns**

> *That* is the fastest route.
> *These* are the best.
> Is *this* what you asked for?

> **NOTE:** The same pronoun sometimes falls into more than one category. To decide how to categorize a pronoun, look at the function it serves in the sentence. For instance, *that* may be a relative pronoun or a demonstrative pronoun.
>
> We did not use the route *that* they recommended. (relative pronoun)
>
> *That* is the route I want to take. (demonstrative pronoun)

Indefinite pronouns refer generally to one or more than one person or thing. The following are some commonly used indefinite pronouns.

**4.A.2.d
Indefinite
Pronouns**

all	either	most	other
any	everybody	neither	several
anybody	everyone	nobody	some
anyone	everything	none	somebody
anything	few	no one	someone
both	many	one	something
each			

> *Somebody* has been here.
> Please pass me a *few*.
> We had to choose from among *several*.

**4.A.2.e
Interrogative
Pronouns**

Interrogative pronouns are pronouns used to ask questions. The interrogative pronouns are *who, which,* and *what.*

> *Who* is going to open the door?
> *Which* of these people have you met?
> *What* is happening over there?

**4.A.2.f
Case of
Pronouns**

Personal pronouns and the pronouns *who* and *whoever* change their form depending upon how they are used in a sentence. These form changes show the *case* of the pronoun. There are three cases: nominative, objective, and possessive.

Nominative Case. A pronoun used as the subject of a sentence is in the *nominative case. See* **4.B.1**: Subjects and Predicates *for more information on subjects.* The nominative pronouns are *I, we, you, he, she, it, they, who, whoever.*

> *You* look tired.
> *We* students complained about the assignment.
> *Who* knows the answer?

> **NOTE:** Many people make mistakes when the subject consists of more than one word. Remember, no matter how many nouns or pronouns are in the subject, the subject is always in the nominative case.
>
> *You* and *she* are invited for dinner. (Not: *You* and *her*)
> *Martin* and *he* went to the game. (Not: *Martin* and *him*)

Pronouns used as predicate nominatives are in the *nominative case. See* **4.A.4.c**: Linking Verbs.

> It was *I* who called.
> Someone left a book on the desk. Was it *you* or *he*?

Objective Case. The objective case pronouns are *me, us, you, him, her, it, them, whom, whomever.*
A pronoun used as the direct object of a verb is in the *objective case. See* **4.A.4.a**: Transitive Verbs *for more about direct objects.*

> Does Mark know that Cathy likes *him*?
> Mother wants *us* to come home for dinner.
> *Whom* will you invite to your party?

A pronoun used as an indirect object is in the *objective case. See* **4.A.4.a**: Transitive Verbs *for more about indirect objects.*

Uncle Charles and Aunt Sarah sent *me* a lovely birthday card.

Would you please tell *us* a story?

Cindy was happy when Dad gave *her* the car keys.

A pronoun used as the object of a preposition is in the *objective case*. <u>*See*</u> **4.A.6**: Prepositions.

Deliver the package directly to *me*, please.

Father is driving to the supermarket. Do you want to go with *him*?

To *whom* do you wish to speak?

Why doesn't anyone ever listen to *us* kids?

NOTE: Many people make mistakes when the direct object, indirect object, and object of a preposition consist of more than one word. Remember, no matter how many nouns or pronouns form the direct object, indirect object, and object of a preposition, they are *all* in the objective case.

If you want to know the answer, just ask *Jack* and *me*.
(*Not: Jack* and *I*)

A good way to test yourself in cases like these is to separate the noun and pronoun. Repeat the sentence using only the pronoun to see which pronoun sounds best. For example, ". . . just ask *me*" sounds much better than ". . . just ask *I*." Therefore, *Jack and me* is correct.

The store never sent *Mother* and *me* the items we ordered.
(*Not: Mother* and *I*)

Martha requested that the survey be sent to *John* and *her*.
(*Not: John* and *she*)

Possessive Case. *Possessive pronouns* indicate ownership. The possessive pronouns are *my, mine, our, ours, your, yours, his, her, hers, its, their, theirs, whose.*

When possessive pronouns are used as predicate nominatives, they use the form *mine, ours, yours, theirs, its, his, hers,* or *whose.*

This book is *mine.*
The yellow sweater is *yours.*

When possessive pronouns are used as adjectives, they take the form *my, our, your, his, her, its, their,* or *whose. See* **4.A.3.b**: Limiting Adjectives *for more about pronominal adjectives.*

This is *my* book.
Whose coat is that?

NOTE: Never use an apostrophe with a possessive pronoun.

The next move is *yours*.
(*Not:* your's)

The wind shifted *its* direction.
(*Not:* it's, which means *it is*)

Whose dog was barking last night?
(*Not:* who's, which means *who is*)

**4.A.2.g
Agreement of
Pronouns**

The noun a pronoun stands for is called a pronoun *antecedent*. A pronoun always agrees with its antecedent in person (first, second, or third), number (singular or plural), and gender (masculine, feminine, or neuter). *See* **4.A.1.a**: Common and Proper Nouns. In the examples, antecedents are marked (A) and pronouns are marked (P).

(A)   (P)
Sally gave *her* crayons to Judy.
(third person, singular, feminine)

┌── (A) ──┐   (P)
Rick and Edna practiced *their* skating routine.
(third person, plural)

(A)   (P)
I am having a hard time with *my* homework tonight.
(first person, singular)

When the antecedent is a collective noun, use either a singular or a plural pronoun, depending upon the meaning of the sentence.

The jury are in the next room casting *their* votes.
(Each member of the jury is casting an individual vote.)

The jury met to reach *its* decision.
(The jury, acting as a unit, met in order to reach a decision.)

NOTE: Formerly, when the antecedent of the pronoun referred to both men and women or when the gender of the antecedent was unknown, the masculine singular pronoun was used.

Each person entering the theater had to show *his* ticket.

However, today many people are reluctant to follow this rule because they feel it arbitrarily assigns roles to people on the basis of sex, fostering sexism in society. The National Council of Teachers of English (NCTE) has issued guidelines to help ensure the use of nonsexist language. The NCTE and other concerned organizations suggest using the plural pronoun.

Each person entering the theater had to show *their* ticket.

But this solution breaks the traditional rule of pronoun/antecedent agreement. Another solution is to use "his or her."

Each person entering the theater had to show *his or her* ticket.

However, this can be awkward. Perhaps the best solution is to rewrite the sentence:

All the people entering the theater had to show *their* tickets.

The indefinite pronouns *anybody, anyone, each, either, everybody, everyone, neither, nobody, no one, one, somebody,* and *someone* are singular.

Each of the girls had *her* own gym locker.
Neither of the boys took *his* turn at bat.

NOTE: Many people make mistakes when plural nouns come between singular indefinite pronouns (which serve as antecedents) and the pronouns that stand for them. Remember, these indefinite pronouns are singular no matter what words follow them.

One of the women lost *her* gloves.
Neither of the men took *his* vacation this year.

4.A.3
Adjectives

An *adjective* is a word that modifies a noun or a pronoun. It makes the meaning of a noun or pronoun more specific by describing or limiting it in some way. The two basic types of adjectives are, thus, descriptive and limiting.

4.A.3.a
Descriptive
Adjectives

A *descriptive adjective* indicates a quality or condition of a noun.

> The area was covered with *thick* vines.
> The plants had *short* roots.
> The trees were surrounded by *red* flowers.
> *High* hills rose in the distance.

4.A.3.b
Limiting
Adjectives

A *limiting adjective* points out a noun or indicates its number or quantity. Limiting adjectives can be classified as numerical adjectives, pronominal adjectives, or articles.

Numerical Adjectives. There are two kinds of numerical adjectives: cardinal and ordinal. *Cardinal adjectives* are numbers that tell how many.

> The manuscript contained *ten* pages.
> *Six* people were in the room.
> The table seats *eight* persons.

Ordinal adjectives are numbers that tell in what order.

> Our team came in *third*.
> The *second* step is broken.
> The *fifth* carbon copy is hard to read.

Pronominal Adjectives. When pronouns are used as adjectives they are known as *pronominal adjectives*. These can be personal, demonstrative, indefinite, or interrogative.

> **Personal:** my, our, your, his, her, their
> Here is *my* garden.
> Welcome to *our* home.
> Where is *your* scarf?
> John was listening to *his* radio.
> Sally lost *her* ring.
> Hank and Phyllis danced to *their* favorite song.

Demonstrative: that, these, those, this
That route is too long.
These colors go well together.
Those people are lost.
This time you've gone too far.

Indefinite: any, few, other, several, somebody
Select *any* dessert you wish.
Few people are as friendly as Martin.
Other methods will work just as well.
Several questions arose.
Somebody from the group should go.

Interrogative: which, what
Which song is number one?
What day will you be available?

Articles. Some grammarians consider both the definite and indefinite articles to be adjectives.

The doctor came to his office.
(definite article)

A number of people complimented me on my baking.
(indefinite article)

Adjectives usually precede the noun or pronoun they modify.

**4.A.3.c
Placement of
Adjectives**

We sat in the *warm* sun.
The *skinny young* man always ate as much as he wanted.

Adjectives may be placed after the noun or pronoun for stylistic variety or special emphasis. In this case, the adjective is in apposition to the noun or pronoun.

The mountain climber, *exhausted,* paused in the shelter.
The dog, *lean* and *alert,* led the search party.

Descriptive adjectives modify nouns and pronouns by indicating their qualities and characteristics. The degree to which nouns and pronouns have a quality or characteristic can be indicated by means of comparison. Adjectives can be compared in ascending (upward) or descending (downward) order.

**4.A.3.d
Comparison of
Adjectives**

There are three degrees of comparison: positive, comparative, and superlative. The *positive degree* expresses the quality or characteristic.

attentive   tall   good

The *comparative degree* expresses a degree higher or lower than the positive.

> more attentive   taller   less tall   better   worse

The *superlative degree* expresses the highest or lowest degree of the quality or characteristic.

> most attentive   tallest   least tall   best   worst

To indicate comparison downward, all adjectives use the words *less* and *least*.

Positive	Comparative	Superlative
tall	less tall	least tall
stubborn	less stubborn	least stubborn
reasonable	less reasonable	least reasonable

There are three ways of forming the comparison upward.

1. Some adjectives add -*er* to form the comparative degree and -*est* for the superlative degree. Almost all adjectives of one syllable and some adjectives of two or more syllables form the comparative this way.

Positive	Comparative	Superlative
tall	taller	tallest
short	shorter	shortest
smart	smarter	smartest
tender	tenderer	tenderest

2. Most adjectives of two or more syllables form the comparative by using the words *more* and *most*.

Positive	Comparative	Superlative
stubborn	more stubborn	most stubborn
attentive	more attentive	most attentive
reasonable	more reasonable	most reasonable

3. Some adjectives form their comparatives irregularly.

Positive	Comparative	Superlative
good/well	better	best
bad/ill	worse	worst
many/much	more	most
far	farther	farthest
little	less	least

NOTE: Never use "more" and "most" when adding the suffixes *-er* and *-est* to adjectives. This is known as a "double comparison" and should be avoided.

Incorrect: Sandra was *more smarter* than Caroline.
Correct: Sandra was *smarter* than Caroline.

Incorrect: Harold is the *most tallest* person I know.
Correct: Harold is the *tallest* person I know.

Adjectives should make descriptions sharper and more interesting. Avoid unnecessary, vague, and repetitious adjectives, which weaken the descriptive power of your writing and speech.

4.A.3.e
Choice of
Adjectives

Unnecessary adjectives:
We visited the observation tower on top of the *tall,* 110-story building.
(Any 110-story building would be tall. Adding the adjective *tall* gives no additional information.)

Vague adjectives:
Debbie is one of the *nicest* people I have ever met.
(The sentence gives no information about what makes Debbie so special. Is she kind? Polite? Helpful? Be specific.)

Repetitious adjectives:
A *big, huge,* truck drove by and splashed water all over my new coat.
(Delete *big* or *huge.* They mean almost the same thing.)

A *predicate adjective* is an adjective that follows a linking verb. Linking verbs include all forms of the verb *to be: am, are, is, was, were.* Other linking verbs include *appear, feel, grow, look, seem, smell, sound,* and *taste.* Such words tell about the subject's state of being. They connect the subject to the adjectives or nouns that follow. *See* **4.A.4.c**: Linking Verbs.

4.A.3.f
Predicate
Adjectives

NOTE: Because many linking verbs can also be used as action verbs (verbs that tell about something that occurs), many people make the mistake of using an adverb after a linking verb. But a modifier following a linking verb is *always* an adjective, *never* an adverb.

Incorrect: That soup tastes *strangely.*
Correct: That soup tastes *strange.*

Incorrect: I feel *badly* when you leave.
Correct: I feel *bad* when you leave.

> **NOTE** *(continued):* To test whether to use an adjective or an adverb, ask, "Which word is being modified?" If the verb is being modified, use an adverb. *See* **4.A.5**: Adverbs. If the subject is being modified, use an adjective.
>
> The children grew *tall.*
> (The adjective *tall* modifies the subject *children.*)
>
> The children grew *quickly.*
> (The adverb *quickly* modifies the verb *grew.*)
>
> Mrs. Johnson appeared *worried* when she heard the news.
> (The adjective *worried* modifies the subject *Mrs. Johnson.*)
>
> Mrs. Johnson appeared *suddenly* from behind the house.
> (The adverb *suddenly* modifies the verb *appeared.*)

COMMON ADJECTIVE ERRORS

This/these and *that/those* are often misused in relation to *kind/kinds* and *sort/sorts.* The pronominal adjective should always agree in number with the noun it modifies.

This (singular) *kind* (singular) of weather.

That (singular) *sort* (singular) of book.

Those (plural) *kinds* (plural) of songs.

These (plural) *sorts* (plural) of exercises.

Never use "a" after *kind of* or *sort of.*

Incorrect: That *sort of a* cake.
Correct: That *sort of* cake.

4.A.4
Verbs

A *verb* is a word that expresses an action or a state of being.

Action verbs express physical and mental actions.

run	talk	sing
think	hope	desire

State of being verbs express a condition or state of being.

appear	be	become	feel	seem

A *transitive verb* expresses action that is performed on something. It may take a direct or an indirect object.

Direct Object. A *direct object* names the person or thing that receives the action of the verb. Each of the following sentences contains a transitive verb that takes a direct object. In the first sentence, the direct object is the noun *ball,* which receives the action of the verb *hits.* In the second sentence, the direct object is the noun *letters,* which receives the action of the verb *write.*

> John *hits* the ball.
> (The ball receives the hitting.)
>
> Margaret *writes* letters to her cousins.
> (The letters receive the writing.)

An easy way to find the direct object in a sentence is to find the subject and verb (*see* **4.B.1**: Subjects and Predicates) and then ask "What?" or "Whom?" In the first sentence, you would ask, "John hit *what?*" In the second, you would ask, "Margaret writes *what?*"

Indirect Object. An *indirect object* names the person or thing to whom or for whom the action of the verb is performed. Each of the following sentences contains both a direct object and an indirect object.

> John threw a *bone* to the *dog.*
> Jennifer sent her *friend* a *letter.*
> Martha gave her *mother* some *perfume.*

In the first sentence, the indirect object is *dog* and the direct object is *bone.* (Ask "John threw *what* to *whom?*") In the second sentence, the indirect object is *friend* and the direct object is *letter.* (Ask "Jennifer sent *what* to *whom?*") In the third sentence, the indirect object is *mother* and the direct object is *perfume.* (Ask "Martha gave *what* to *whom?*")

An *intransitive verb* is a verb that does not take a direct object. Each of the following example sentences contains an intransitive verb.

> Mark *sings* in the school choir.
> Harriet *walks* in the woods.
> Our baby brother *sleeps* through the night.

TRANSITIVE OR INTRANSITIVE?

Many verbs can be either transitive or intransitive, depending upon how they are used in the sentence. Remember: if a verb takes a direct object, it is a transitive verb. If it does not take a direct object, it is an intransitive verb.

Mary *writes* a letter.
(transitive—the direct object is *letter*)

Mary *writes* beautifully.
(intransitive—no direct object)

John *walked* his dog.
(transitive—the direct object is *dog*)

John *walked* to the store.
(intransitive—no direct object)

I *read* three books a week.
(transitive—the direct object is *books*)

I *read* quickly.
(intransitive—no direct object)

**4.A.4.c
Linking Verbs**

A *linking verb* is an intransitive, state-of-being verb that requires an adjective or a noun or pronoun to complete its meaning. The most common linking verb is the verb *to be* in all its forms: *am, are, is, was, were.* Some other common linking verbs are *act, appear, feel, grow, look, seem, sound, taste,* and *turn.*

Each of the following sentences contains a linking verb, and each sentence tells about a state of being. The verbs—*seems, feel, smells, is*—link the subjects of the sentences with the adjectives or nouns that describe them.

Jack *seems* sad.
I *feel* bad.
The chocolate cake baking in the oven *smells* delicious.
That man in the gray hat *is* our lawyer.

NOTE: Most linking verbs can also be used as action verbs (verbs that express physical or mental action).

Linking verb: The hour *grew* late.
Harold *appeared* satisfied.

Action verb: The children *grew* quickly.
Mrs. Robinson *appeared* at the door.

NOTE: The adjectives or nouns that follow linking verbs are very closely related to the subjects of the linking verbs. In fact, they describe, define, or explain the subject. Adjectives that follow linking verbs are called *predicate adjectives*. Nouns or pronouns that follow linking verbs are called *predicate nominatives*.

Joyce looks *pretty*.
(predicate adjective)

The radio sounds *funny*.
(predicate adjective)

Clarence became a *doctor*.
(predicate nominative)

Marsha was a *leader*.
(predicate nominative)

For more information, *see* **4.A.3.f**: Predicate Adjectives.

4.A.4.d
Voice

All transitive verbs may have two voices: active or passive. In the *active voice*, the subject of the verb performs the action. In the *passive voice*, the subject of the verb receives the action.

John hit the ball.
(active voice; subject—John)

The ball was hit by John.
(passive voice; subject—ball)

A local company performed the opera.
(active voice; subject—company)

The opera was performed by a local company.
(passive voice; subject—opera)

Notice what has happened in the preceding four sentences. *Ball,* the direct object in the first sentence, has become the subject in the second sentence. *Opera,* the direct object in the third sentence, has become the subject in the fourth sentence. You may transform sentences from the active voice to the passive voice by turning the direct object into the subject.

Form the passive voice by using the appropriate form of the verb *to be,* plus the past participle of the principal verb.

The ball *is hit*.
The ball *was hit*.
The ball *will be hit*.
The ball *will have been hit*.

4.A.4.e
Mood

The *mood* of a verb indicates the attitude or viewpoint behind the verb's expression. There are three moods: *indicative, imperative,* and *subjunctive.*

The *indicative mood* indicates a statement or question of fact.

That man *is* my uncle.
Ned *knows* how to tap dance.
Did you *see* the beautiful antique cars on display?

The *imperative mood* indicates a request or a command.

Take it easy.
Come here, please.
Finish your homework before you go out.

The *subjunctive mood* indicates that the action or state of being is doubtful, conditional, unreal, or improbable. *See* **5.C.4.f**: Subjunctive Mood.

If I *were* you, I would be more careful.

Should you *care* to reconsider, Mr. Brown will be happy to speak with you.

4.A.4.f
Person and
Number

The *person* of a verb indicates whether the verb refers to the person speaking (first person), the person spoken to (second person), or the person spoken about (third person).

First person	Second person	Third person
I go	you go	he goes
I walk	you walk	she walks
we see	you see	it sees

The *number* of a verb indicates whether the verb refers to a singular or a plural subject.

Singular	Plural
I go	we go
you go	you go
he goes	they go

In almost all verbs, only the third person singular changes form to indicate person and number.

The *tense* of a verb indicates the time of the verb's action. There are three major divisions of time: past, present, and future. In each of these time frames, the action may be considered as simple (simply occurring at the particular moment) or perfect (the action is completed or "perfected").

There are thus six tenses in English: present, present perfect, past, past perfect, future, and future perfect.

4.A.4.g
Tense

1. **The present tense:**
    ■ indicates action occurring in the present.

    I *see* my sister playing in the schoolyard.
    The fire fighters *hear* the alarm and *spring* into action.

    ■ indicates habitual or customary action.

    Jim *walks* his dog every morning before school.
    My brother *talks* in his sleep.

    ■ indicates unchanging conditions, facts, or beliefs.

    One plus one *equals* two.
    Congressional elections *are held* every two years.
    When it *rains* it *pours*.

    ■ indicates action completed in the past. (This is called the historical present and is used when the writer or speaker wants to make an especially vivid impression.)

    Then, on December 16, about 45 Bostonians dressed as Indians *raid* three British ships and *throw* 340 chests of tea into Boston Harbor. The Revolutionary War in America *is* coming closer now. It finally *begins* on April 19, 1775. This time, the place *is* Lexington, Massachusetts.

    ■ indicates action that will occur.

    She *flies* to Houston tomorrow.
    He *signs* the contract next week.

2. **The present perfect tense:**
   - indicates action begun in the past and completed by the present moment.

     Jerry *has taken* all the required courses.
     I *have seen* the play that was recently reviewed in the *Daily Chronicle.*

   - indicates action begun in the past and continuing up to or through the present moment.

     Cynthia *has been* my friend since the first day she moved to town.

     Harry *has been* shooting baskets for at least half an hour.

3. **The past tense:**
   - indicates action completed in the past.

     We *went* to the movies yesterday.
     I *enjoyed* meeting your cousin.

4. **The past perfect tense:**
   - indicates an action that occurred in the past prior to another past action or event.

     Mark *had finished* drying the dishes by the time Sam arrived.

     I *had heard* good things about you long before I met you.

5. **The future tense:**
   - indicates an action that will occur in the future.

     They *will call* you later this afternoon.
     Martin *will visit* his aunt next month.

6. **The future perfect tense:**
   - indicates an action that will be completed at some future time.

     Sandra *will have finished* two years of college by the time you see her this summer.

     We *will* already *have left* for our vacation before Saturday.

CONSISTENCY OF TENSE

Be sure that the tenses of all verbs in a sentence are consistent with one another. All actions occurring at the same time should be in the same tense.

Incorrect: John *walked* into study hall and *starts* complaining about his grade on the spelling test.

Correct: John *walked* into study hall and *started* complaining about his grade on the spelling test.

Sometimes sentences describe a number of actions occurring at different times. Make sure the tenses represent the sequence of events correctly.

Incorrect: He already *left* by the time I *arrived*.
Correct: He *had* already *left* by the time I *arrived*.

Incorrect: Elaine *has promised* to call when she *got* home.
Correct: Elaine *has promised* to call when she *gets* home.

Frequently, two or more verbs are required to indicate tense, voice, and mood. These groups of two or more verbs are called *verb phrases*. Verb phrases consist of a form of the principal verb plus one or more auxiliary, or "helping," verbs.

4.A.4.h
Verb Phrases

> I *will go* to the store this afternoon.
> The game *was enjoyed* by all.
> I *might decide* not to go.

Principal Verb. In verb phrases, the principal verb usually takes the form of the present participle or the past participle. The present participle of a verb ends in *-ing*.

> *seeing*   *hearing*   *speaking*

The past participle of a verb ends in *-d, -ed, -t, -en,* or *-n*.

> *walked*   *left*   *stolen*

Auxiliary Verbs. The most common auxiliary or helping verbs are *be, can, could, do, have, may, might, must, shall, should, will,* and *would*. (*Be, do,* and *have* can also function as principal verbs. For instance: "I am a student"; "You do your best"; "We have three books." The other auxiliary verbs, such as *could, might, should,* and *would,* are sometimes called "modal verbs.")

NOTE: The entire verb phrase is considered to be the verb.

I *have seen* the Grand Canyon.
I *will have finished* my book report by Friday.

Word placement has no effect on what constitutes the verb.

I *will* certainly *have decided* by Friday.
(The verb is *will have decided*.)

4.A.4.i
Principal Parts
of Verbs

Every verb has three principal parts: the present infinitive (usually called "the present"), the past indicative (usually called "the past"), and the past participle. Regular verbs form the past and the past participle by adding *-d* or *-ed* to the present infinitive.

Present	Past	Past participle
walk	walked	walked
look	looked	looked
dance	danced	danced
close	closed	closed

Verbs that form the past tense and/or the past participle in any other way are called irregular verbs.

Present	Past	Past participle
eat	ate	eaten
sit	sat	sat
speak	spoke	spoken
write	wrote	written
mean	meant	meant

Most dictionaries give the principal parts of irregular verbs. The principal parts of regular verbs are not listed. *See* **2.G**: Using a Dictionary. Following is a list of the principal parts of some of the most common irregular verbs.

Principal Parts of Common Irregular Verbs

PRESENT	PAST	PAST PARTICIPLE
be	was	been
beat	beat	beaten
become	became	become
begin	began	begun
bend	bent	bent
bind	bound	bound
blow	blew	blown
break	broke	broken
bring	brought	brought
build	built	built
burn	burned/burnt	burned/burnt
buy	bought	bought
catch	caught	caught
choose	chose	chosen
come	came	come
dive	dived/dove	dived
do	did	done
draw	drew	drawn
drink	drank	drunk
drive	drove	driven
eat	ate	eaten
fall	fell	fallen
fight	fought	fought
flee	fled	fled
fly	flew	flown
forbid	forbade	forbidden
freeze	froze	frozen
get	got	got/gotten
give	gave	given
go	went	gone
grow	grew	grown
hang (suspend)	hung	hung
hang (execute)	hanged	hanged
hide	hid	hidden/hid
hold	held	held
know	knew	known
lay (put or place)	laid	laid
lead	led	led
lend	lent	lent
let	let	let
lie (recline; remain in position)	lay	lain
lie (tell a lie)	lied	lied
lose	lost	lost
make	made	made
mean	meant	meant

PRESENT	PAST	PAST PARTICIPLE
pay	paid	paid
quit	quit	quit
ride	rode	ridden
ring	rang	rung
rise	rose	risen
run	ran	run
say	said	said
see	saw	seen
set (put or place)	set	set
shake	shook	shaken
shrink	shrank/shrunk	shrunk/shrunken
sing	sang	sung
sink	sank	sunk
sit (remain in upright position)	sat	sat
sling	slung	slung
sow	sowed	sown/sowed
speak	spoke	spoken
spring	sprang	sprung
steal	stole	stolen
sting	stung	stung
swear	swore	sworn
swim	swam	swum
swing	swung	swung
take	took	taken
teach	taught	taught
tear	tore	torn
throw	threw	thrown
wake	woke/waked	waked/woken
wear	wore	worn
weave	wove	woven
wring	wrung	wrung
write	wrote	written

4.A.4.j Conjugation

The conjugation of a verb is the orderly presentation of all its forms to indicate tense, voice, mood, number, and person. All the forms of a verb can be derived from its three principal parts (present, past, and past participle) combined with any necessary auxiliary verbs.

Complete Conjugation of the Active Voice of *to See*

INDICATIVE MOOD			
SINGULAR	**PLURAL**	**SINGULAR**	**PLURAL**
Present tense		**Present perfect tense**	
I see	we see	I have seen	we have seen
you see	you see	you have seen	you have seen
he, she, it sees	they see	he, she, it has seen	they have seen
Past tense		**Past perfect tense**	
I saw	we saw	I had seen	we had seen
you saw	you saw	you had seen	you had seen
he, she, it saw	they saw	he, she, it had seen	they had seen
Future tense		**Future perfect tense**	
I shall see	we shall see	I shall have seen	we shall have seen
you will see	you will see	you will have seen	you will have seen
he, she, it will see	they will see	he, she, it will have seen	they will have seen

SUBJUNCTIVE MOOD			
SINGULAR	**PLURAL**	**SINGULAR**	**PLURAL**
Present tense		**Present perfect tense**	
(if) I see	(if) we see	(if) I have seen	(if) we have seen
(if) you see	(if) you see	(if) you have seen	(if) you have seen
(if) he, she, it sees	(if) they see	(if) he, she, it has seen	(if) they have seen
Past tense		**Past perfect tense**	
(if) I saw	(if) we saw	(if) I had seen	(if) we had seen
(if) you saw	(if) you saw	(if) you had seen	(if) you had seen
(if) he, she, it saw	(if) they saw	(if) he, she, it had seen	(if) they had seen
(if) you saw	(if) you saw	(if) you had seen	(if) you had seen
Future tense		**Future perfect tense**	
(if) I should see	(if) we should see	(if) I should have seen	(if) we should have seen
(if) you should see	(if) you should see	(if) you should have seen	(if) you should have seen
(if) he, she, it should see	(if) they should see	(if) he, she, it should have seen	(if) they should have seen

IMPERATIVE MOOD			
(you) See—singular and plural			
	PRESENT	**PAST**	**PERFECT**
Infinitive forms:	to see		to have seen
Participles:	seeing	seen	having seen
Gerunds:	seeing		having seen

For a discussion of infinitive forms, participles, and gerunds, *see* **4.A.4.k**: Verbals.

A synopsis of a conjugation is a presentation of a verb's conjugation in one person and one number.

Synopsis of the Passive Voice of *to See,* First Person Singular.

INDICATIVE MOOD	
Present tense:	I am seen
Past tense:	I was seen
Future tense:	I shall be seen
Present perfect tense:	I have been seen
Past perfect tense:	I had been seen
Future perfect tense:	I shall have been seen
SUBJUNCTIVE MOOD	
Present tense:	(if) I be seen
Past tense:	(if) I were seen
Future tense:	(if) I should be seen
Present perfect tense:	(if) I have been seen
Past perfect tense:	(if) I had been seen
Future perfect tense:	(if) I should have been seen
IMPERATIVE MOOD	
(You) Be seen—singular and plural	

All the preceding conjugations are *simple conjugations.* Another important conjugation is the *progressive conjugation,* which shows continuous action.

Synopsis of the Progressive Conjugation of *to See*, Active Voice, First Person Singular

INDICATIVE MOOD	
Present tense:	I am seeing
Past tense:	I was seeing
Future tense:	I shall be seeing
Present perfect tense:	I have been seeing
Past perfect tense:	I had been seeing
Future perfect tense:	I shall have been seeing

SUBJUNCTIVE MOOD	
Present tense:	(if) I be seeing (usage confined to poetry and certain idioms)
Past tense:	(if) I were seeing
Future tense:	(if) I should be seeing
Present perfect tense:	(if) I have been seeing
Past perfect tense:	(if) I had been seeing
Future perfect tense	(if) I should have been seeing

IMPERATIVE MOOD
(You) Be seeing—singular and plural

NOTE: Do not confuse verb phrases in the progressive conjugation with the present participle used as an adjective.

I *am singing.*
(verb phrase in progressive conjugation)

The *singing* bird nested in the tree.
(present participle used as adjective)

Verbals are verb forms that function as parts of speech other than verbs while retaining some characteristics of verbs. There are three kinds of verbals: infinitives, participles, and gerunds.

The Infinitive. The *infinitive* is the basic form of the verb. It acts as a verbal when it is preceded by the preposition *to* (for example, *to walk, to go, to see*). An infinitive may be used as a noun, an adjective, or an adverb.

As a noun:
To err is human.
(infinitive used as the subject of a sentence)

I want *to go.*
(infinitive used as a direct object)

Her main goal, *to win,* is unrealistic.
(infinitive used as an appositive)

As an adjective:
Here is a book *to read*.
(infinitive used to modify the noun *book*)

Our vacation was a time *to relax*.
(infinitive used to modify the predicate nominative *time*)

As an adverb:
That is easy *to say*.
(infinitive used to modify the predicate adjective *easy*)

John played *to win*.
(infinitive used to modify the verb *played*)

Notice that although the infinitive functions as a noun and is the subject of the sentence in the following examples, it retains some of the characteristics of a verb. For instance, it can take a direct object or it can be modified by an adverb.

To play the piano was his greatest desire.
(infinitive: *to play*; direct object: *piano*)

To run quickly is difficult.
(infinitive: *to run*; adverb *quickly*)

The Participle. Every verb has both a present participle and a past participle. The present participle always ends in *-ing*.

singing   dancing

The past participle usually ends in *-ed, -d, -t, -en,* or *-n*.

walked   chosen

Participles have two uses. Sometimes they are used to make verb phrases.

I *am singing*; you *had gone*.

Sometimes they are used as adjectives. It is when participles act as adjectives that they are classified as verbals.

Carole calmed the *frightened* kitten.
(past participle used as an adjective)

Do you like *baked* potatoes?
(past participle used as an adjective)

Burning leaves smell good.
(present participle used as an adjective)

The *chirping* birds woke us up early.
(present participle used as an adjective)

Although the past and present participles function as adjectives, they retain some of the characteristics of verbs. For instance, they can take an object, and they can be modified by an adverb.

The girl *painting the fence* is my sister.
(present participle: *painting*; direct object: *fence*)

Bowing modestly, the violinist acknowledged the audience's applause.
(present participle: *bowing*; adverb: *modestly*)

The Gerund. A gerund is a verb form ending in *-ing* that functions as a noun.

Swimming is good exercise.
(gerund acting as the subject)

I enjoy *hiking*.
(gerund acting as a direct object)

My favorite sport, *fencing,* keeps me in shape.
(gerund acting as an appositive)

Although the gerund functions as a noun, it retains some of the characteristics of a verb. For instance, it can take an object, and it can be modified by an adverb.

I enjoy *singing folk songs*.
(gerund: *singing*; object: *folk songs*)

Walking briskly is healthful.
(gerund: *walking*; adverb: *briskly*)

Gerunds and present participles used as adjectives both have *-ing* endings. Be careful not to confuse them when analyzing their function in a sentence.

I like *swimming*.
(gerund used as a noun)

The *swimming* children frolicked in the pool.
(present participle used as an adjective)

Verbs must agree in number with their subjects. *See* **5.B.1.a:** Subject-Verb Agreement.

**4.A.4.l
Agreement of
Verbs**

Harry runs a mile a day.
(third person singular subject: *Harry*
third person singular verb: *runs*)

We go to the store after school.
(first person plural subject: *We*
first person plural verb: *go*)

Singular verbs are used with the following indefinite pronouns: *anybody, anyone, each, either, every, everybody, everyone, neither, nobody, no one, one, somebody,* and *someone.*

> *Each* apartment *has* its own separate heating unit.
> *Neither* boy *wants* to run the errand.

Singular verbs are used with these pronouns even when the pronouns and the verbs are separated by phrases or clauses containing plural nouns.

> *Each* of the apartments *has* its own separate heating unit.
> *Neither* of the boys *wants* to run the errand.

Compound subjects (two or more nouns used as the subject) usually take a plural verb. *See* **4.B.1**: Subjects and Predicates.

> *Melissa and Charles plan* to be married in June.
> *Mother and Father go* out every Saturday night.
> *Sue, Donna, and Ellen are* on the soccer team.

When the parts of a compound subject are thought of as one unit, they take a singular verb.

> *Peanut butter and jelly is* my favorite sandwich spread.
> *The hustle and bustle* of traffic *is* getting on my nerves.

Compound subjects joined by the words *or, either . . . or,* and *neither . . . nor* take a singular verb unless the second subject is plural.

> Either Becky or Linda *wins* every prize.
> Neither Harry nor Cathy *wants* to dry the dishes.
> Sam or Kevin *has* the key.
> Jenny or the boys *have* the car.

4.A.5 Adverbs

An *adverb* is a word that modifies a verb, an adjective, or another adverb.

4.A.5.a Types of Adverbs

Adverbs usually answer the question How? When? Where? or To what extent?

> Mark walked *slowly.*
> (*Slowly* modifies the verb *walked* and tells *how*.)
>
> I will leave *soon.*
> (*Soon* modifies the verb *leave* and tells *when*)
>
> Let's go *out.*
> (*Out* modifies the verb *go* and tells *where.*)
>
> Sally is *not* late.
> (*Not* modifies the adjective *late* and tells *to what extent.*)

The elderly man moved *quite* gingerly.
(*Quite* modifies the adverb *gingerly* and tells *to what extent*.)

Classifying Adverbs by Meaning. Adverbs that tell how are called *adverbs of manner*.

beautifully   energetically   happily   quickly   fast

Adverbs that tell when are called *adverbs of time*.

now   soon   then   before   later

Adverbs that tell where are called *adverbs of place*.

in   out   near   up   down   forward   there

Some adverbs of place can also function as prepositions. *See* the first note for **4.A.6**: Prepositions.

Let's climb *up*.
(adverb)

The kitten climbed *up* the tree.
(preposition)

Adverbs that tell to what extent are called *adverbs of degree*.

very   extremely   rather   somewhat   quite   almost

Classifying Adverbs by Function. *Interrogative adverbs* introduce questions.

When did you go?
Where have you been?
How did Tasha know that?
Why did you leave the door open?

Relative adverbs introduce dependent (subordinate) clauses.

I will meet you *when* classes are over.
Do you know *why* Max was so angry?
I don't know *where* I left my keys.

Conjunctive adverbs (sometimes called *transitional adverbs*) join two independent clauses or two sentences and modify one of them. *See* **4.B.4**: Clauses.

hence	moreover	otherwise	therefore
however	nevertheless	still	thus

We followed the recipe; *however,* the casserole was not as good as we'd hoped.

Sarah liked the dress; *nevertheless,* she did not buy it.

Independent adverbs have no grammatical function in the sentence or clause.

No, I don't think I'll join you.
Yes, you did leave your gloves at the skating rink.

**4.A.5.b
Comparison of
Adverbs**

Adverbs of manner (adverbs that tell how), like adjectives, may be compared upward and downward in three degrees: positive, comparative, and superlative.

1. Most adverbs are compared upward by using "more" for the comparative degree and "most" for the superlative degree.

POSITIVE	COMPARATIVE	SUPERLATIVE
happily	more happily	most happily
quickly	more quickly	most quickly
accurately	more accurately	most accurately

2. A few adverbs are compared upward by using *-er* for the comparative degree and *-est* for the superlative degree.

POSITIVE	COMPARATIVE	SUPERLATIVE
soon	sooner	soonest
near	nearer	nearest
early	earlier	earliest

3. All adverbs are compared downward by using "less" for the comparative degree and "least" for the superlative degree.

POSITIVE	COMPARATIVE	SUPERLATIVE
early	less early	least early
happily	less happily	least happily
quickly	less quickly	least quickly
accurately	less accurately	least accurately

4. Some adverbs are compared irregularly.

POSITIVE	COMPARATIVE	SUPERLATIVE
badly	worse	worst
far	farther	farthest
	further	furthest
little	less	least
much	more	most
well	better	best

ADVERB OR ADJECTIVE?

Many words that end in *-ly* are adverbs.

> surely   strongly   sharply

However, some words that end in *-ly* are adjectives.

> lovely   manly   friendly   cowardly

And some adverbs do not end in *-ly*.

> here   there   far   soon   fast

Some words can be used as either adverbs or adjectives.

WORD	ADVERB	ADJECTIVE
deep	Dig *deep* to find water.	We dug a *deep* well.
far	We walked *far* into the forest.	He came from a *far* country.
hard	Mark hit the ball *hard*.	It was a *hard* choice.
little, long	The world will *little* note nor *long* remember . . .	He had *little* feet and *long* legs.
near	The horse came *near*.	It was a *near* escape.
right	Turn *right* at the stop sign.	That was the *right* way to turn.
straight	He drew his lines *straight*.	He walked a *straight* line.

Other words that can be used as either adverbs or adjectives include *close, daily, first, hard, high, late, only, tight*.

To test whether a word is an adverb or an adjective, look at how it is used in the sentence. If it modifies a noun, it is an adjective. If it modifies a verb, adjective, or other adverb, it is an adverb.

> There goes Marsha on her *daily* trip to the store.
> (*Daily* is an adjective modifying the noun *trip*.)

> Marsha goes to the store *daily*.
> (*Daily* is an adverb modifying the verb *goes*.)

Some words have two closely related adverb forms:

cheap—cheaply	near—nearly
deep—deeply	quick—quickly
hard—hardly	right—rightly
high—highly	slow—slowly

ADVERB OR ADJECTIVE?

In some cases, usually in short commands, the two forms have the same meaning and can be used interchangeably. The shorter form is considered to be more informal.

Go *slow* around that curve.
Go *slowly* around that curve.

In other cases, the two forms have different meanings and cannot be used interchangeably.

Sam hit the ball *hard*.

Nancy *hardly* had time to catch her breath before she had to go out.

Come sit *near* me.

You *nearly* missed that turnpike exit.

**4.A.5.c
Placement of
Adverbs**

Since adverbs may modify verbs, adjectives, and other adverbs, they may appear in many different positions in a sentence. The meaning of a sentence may vary depending on where the adverb is placed.

Jack *almost* caught a dozen fish this morning.
(Jack came very close to catching a dozen fish.)

Jack caught *almost* a dozen fish this morning.
(Jack caught somewhat fewer than twelve fish.)

I *just* spoke with Sally.
(I spoke with Sally only a few minutes ago.)

I spoke *just* with Sally.
(Sally was the only person with whom I spoke.)

NOTE: Be especially careful about the placement of adverbs such as *almost, only, just, even, hardly, scarcely, merely,* and *nearly.* Place these adverbs as close as possible to the words they modify so as to clarify the meaning of the sentence.

A *preposition* is a word or group of words that shows the relationship of a noun or pronoun to some other word in the sentence.

> The fish swam *in* the tank.
> (The preposition *in* shows the relationship between the noun *tank* and the verb *swam*.)
>
> The boy running *with* his dog slipped and fell.
> (The preposition *with* shows the relationship between the noun *dog* and the participle *running*.)
>
> Sandra hung her coat *on* the hook.
> (The preposition *on* shows the relationship between the noun *hook* and the noun *coat*.)
>
> We were talking *about* you.
> (The preposition *about* shows the relationship between the pronoun *you* and the verb *were talking*.)

Following is a list of some of the most frequently used prepositions.

about	beneath	off
above	beside	on
across	between	out
after	by	over
against	down	throughout
around	during	to
as far as	except	toward
at	for	under
because of	from	until
before	in	up
behind	in spite of	with
below	of	

Object of the Preposition. The *object of the preposition* is the noun or pronoun that follows the preposition and whose relationship to another word is shown by the preposition.

> What do you think about his *idea*?
> (The noun *idea* is the object of the preposition *about*.)
>
> Harold loves hamburgers broiled on the *grill*.
> (The noun *grill* is the object of the preposition *on*.)
>
> Come sit beside *me*.
> (The pronoun *me* is the object of the preposition *beside*.)

GRAMMAR

PREPOSITION OR ADVERB?

Many words that function as prepositions can also function as adverbs. For example:

The cat ran *out* the door.
(*Out* functions as a preposition, taking the object *door*.)
The cat ran *out*.
(*Out* functions as an adverb, modifying the verb *ran*.)

We stumbled *down* the hill.
(*Down* functions as a preposition, taking the object *hill*.)
We stumbled *down*.
(*Down* functions as an adverb, modifying the verb *stumbled*.)

The smoke drifted *up* the chimney.
(*Up* functions as a preposition, taking the object *chimney*.)
The smoke drifted *up*.
(*Up* functions as an adverb, modifying the verb *drifted*.)

In cases like these, to tell whether the word functions as a preposition or an adverb, test to see if it takes an object. If it does, it functions as a preposition. If it does not, it functions as an adverb.

WHICH PREPOSITION TO USE?

Specific prepositions are often closely associated with other nouns, adjectives, and verbs.

account for	foreign to	protest against
argue with	happy about	sensitive to
capable of	independent of	similar to
confide in	inseparable from	sympathize with
desirous of	obedient to	tamper with
envious of		

The same word may sometimes be associated with several different prepositions. In this case, each preposition provides a slightly different shade of meaning:

angry at	careless about	free from
angry with	careless of	free of
apply for	concerned for	part from
apply to	concerned with	part with

WHICH PREPOSITION TO USE?

In a good dictionary, the entry for the principal word will explain the subtle differences in meaning created by using different prepositions. *See* **2.G**: Using a Dictionary.

When two or more words associated with different prepositions appear before one object, do not delete any of the prepositions.

Charlie was *interested in* and *curious about* local politics.

When two or more words associated with the same preposition appear before one object, all but the last preposition may be deleted.

Charlie was *interested* and *involved in* local politics.

A *conjunction* joins words, phrases, clauses, or sentences. There are three kinds of conjunctions: coordinating, subordinating, and correlative.

4.A.7
Conjunctions

Coordinating conjunctions join sentence elements that have the same grammatical value—words with words; phrases with phrases; clauses with clauses; and sentences with sentences. *See* **4.B**: Parts of a Sentence. The most common coordinating conjunctions are *and, but, for, or, nor, yet,* and *so.*

4.A.7.a
Coordinating
Conjunctions

Words with words: Samantha will play basketball *or* baseball.
(The coordinating conjunction *or* joins the two nouns *basketball* and *baseball*.)

Phrases with phrases: Andy sat on the bench strumming his guitar *and* humming a tune.
(The coordinating conjunction *and* joins the two participial phrases *strumming his guitar* and *humming a tune*.)

Subordinate clauses with subordinate clauses: That is the woman who works in the bakery *but* who hates sweets.
(The coordinating conjunction *but* joins the two subordinate clauses *who works in the bakery* and *who hates sweets*.

Sentences with sentences: Our team members vowed to win the trophy. *Yet* they failed.
(The coordinating conjunction *yet* joins the two sentences, *Our team members vowed to win the trophy* and *They failed*)

4.A.7.b
Subordinating
Conjunctions

Subordinating conjunctions connect subordinate clauses to main clauses. *See* **4.B.4**:Clauses. The most common subordinating conjunctions include:

after	how	till
although	if	unless
as	in order that	when
as if	since	where
because	so that	while
before	that	why
but	though	

We will meet for practice on the field tomorrow *unless* it rains.
(The subordinating conjunction *unless* connects the subordinate clause, *unless it rains,* to the main clause.)

You must finish your homework *if* you want to go out.
(The subordinating conjunction *if* connects the subordinate clause, *if you want to go out,* to the main clause.)

4.A.7.c
Correlative
Conjunctions

Correlative conjunctions are two coordinating conjunctions used as a pair. Some common correlative conjunctions are *both . . . and, not only . . . but also, either . . . or, whether . . . or, neither . . . nor.*

Marsha had *neither* the time *nor* the patience to listen to Judy's complaints.

We couldn't decide *whether* to stay *or* to go.

Placement of Correlative Conjunctions. Place correlative conjunctions where they will clearly join the words you wish to connect.

Unclear:	Mark both likes Monica and Sandy.
Clear:	Mark likes both Monica and Sandy.
Unclear:	Randy not only got A's in math but in English, too.
Clear:	Randy got A's not only in math but in English, too.

Elements Joined by Correlative Conjunctions. Make sure you use correlative conjunctions to join sentence elements that are similar—nouns with nouns, adjectives with adjectives, prepositional phrases with prepositional phrases, and so forth.

Incorrect:	Rita is both talented and makes friends easily.
Correct:	Rita is both talented and likeable.

Incorrect: We went not only to the bank but also grocery shopping.

Correct: We went not only to the bank but also to the grocery store.

An *interjection* is a word or phrase that expresses emotion. Interjections have no grammatical connection with the other words in a sentence.

Interjections that express strong emotion are set off by an exclamation point. Interjections that express mild emotion are set off by a comma. *See* **6.B**: Punctuation.

Commonly used interjections include *bravo, hurrah, oh, ouch,* and *whoops*.

Watch out! You almost drove through a stop sign.
Oh, never mind.

4.A.8
Interjections

NOTE: Interjections are used more frequently in spoken than in written language. Use interjections sparingly in your writing. Too many interjections will dull the very impact you are trying to create.

The sentence is an important building block of communication. A *sentence* is a group of words that contains a subject and a predicate and expresses a complete thought.

4.B

Parts of a Sentence

NOTE: Fully understanding the definition of a sentence can help you to write better sentences. *See also* **Chapter 5**: Usage and Style *and* **7.D**: Editing.

The *subject* is the part of a sentence about which something is said. The *predicate* is the part of a sentence that says something about the subject.

4.B.1
Subjects and Predicates

I / like strawberries.
subject / predicate

The bright summer sun / filtered through the trees.
subject / predicate

In most cases, the subject precedes the predicate. In some cases, however, the subject follows the predicate.

> Up and away flew / the kite.
>   predicate / subject

> In the mailbox was / the letter we'd been waiting for.
>   predicate / subject

There are two ways of looking at the subject and predicate of a sentence. One way is to look at the complete subject and predicate. The other way is to look at the simple subject and predicate.

The *simple subject* is the noun or pronoun about which something is said.

The *complete subject* consists of the simple subject and all the words associated with it.

> The cheerful little girl / played baseball in the park.
> Simple subject: girl
> Complete subject: the cheerful little girl

> The tall glass building / reflected the sunlight.
> Simple subject: building
> Complete subject: the tall glass building

> The sticky black mud / covered the sidewalk.
> Simple subject: mud
> Complete subject: the sticky black mud

When teachers refer to the subject of a sentence, they are usually referring to the simple subject. The *simple predicate* is the verb that says something about the subject. The *complete predicate* consists of the verb and all the words associated with it.

> The track team / ran at a slow pace.
> Simple predicate: ran
> Complete predicate: ran at a slow pace

> The eagle / rose from the nest with stately grace.
> Simple predicate: rose
> Complete predicate: rose from the nest with stately grace

> The car / spun out of control on the turn.
> Simple predicate: spun
> Complete predicate: spun out of control on the turn

**4.B.1.a
Compound
Subjects**

A *compound subject* consists of two or more nouns or pronouns that are the subject of the same verb.

> *Sandra* and *Jim* went to the movies.
> *Cathy, Max,* and *I* are running for class president.

A *compound predicate* consists of two or more verbs that have the same subject.

> Richard *danced* and *sang* in the school play.
> The soda *bubbled* and *fizzed* in the glass.

In addition to containing a subject and a predicate, a sentence must express a complete thought. If it does not, it is called a *sentence fragment*. Following are some examples of sentence fragments.

> the tree along the path
> (This is a sentence fragment because it contains no predicate.)
>
> ran toward the lake
> (This is a sentence fragment because it contains no subject.)
>
> If I win the contest
> (This is a sentence fragment because it does not express a complete thought, even though it contains both a subject and a predicate.)

A *phrase* is a group of two or more related words that does not contain both a subject and a predicate. A phrase is used in place of single words in a sentence. Improper placement of a phrases results in dangling modifiers. *See* **5.B.7**: Problems with Modifiers.

A *prepositional phrase* contains a preposition, its objects, and any modifiers. *See* **4.A.6**: Prepositions.

> in the sunny garden
> after my arrival
> by the cool fountain

Prepositional phrases are used as adjectives or adverbs.

> **As an adjective**:
> The man *in the gray hat* is my father.
> (The prepositional phrase modifies the noun *man*.)
>
> Do you shop at that store *on the corner*?
> (The prepositional phrase modifies the noun *store*.)
>
> **As an adverb**:
> Don't talk *with your mouth full*.
> (The prepositional phrase modifies the verb *talk*.)
>
> We arrived *after the intermission*.
> (The prepositional phrase modifies the verb *arrived*.)

**4.B.3.b
Participial
Phrases**

A *participial phrase* contains a present or past participle, its objects, and any modifiers (present participles end in *-ing*; past participles end in *-ed*). *See* **4.A.4.k**: Verbals.

working at his sloppy desk   surprised at the news
singing songs   locked from within

Participial phrases are used as adjectives.

Do you see that girl *playing in the yard*?
(The participial phrase modifies the noun *girl*.)

Frightened by the horror movie, Fred was unable to fall asleep.
(The participial phrase modifies the proper noun *Fred*.)

**4.B.3.c
Gerund Phrases**

A *gerund phrase* contains a gerund, its objects, and any modifiers. Gerund phrases look exactly like participial phrases; they are formed the same way. The difference between participial phrases and gerund phrases has to do with their functions in sentences where they are used. *See* **4.A.4.k**. Verbals.

Gerund phrases are used as nouns.

Driving on mountain roads demands special concentration.
(The gerund phrase is the subject of the verb *demands*.)

I enjoy *taking long walks in the country*.
(The gerund phrase is the object of the verb *enjoy*.)

NOTE: Do not confuse gerund phrases and participial phrases. Gerund phrases are used as nouns; participial phrases are used as adjectives.

Swimming laps takes stamina.
(The gerund phrase is the subject of the verb *takes*.)

The girl *swimming laps* is my sister.
(The participial phrase modifies the noun *girl*.)

**4.B.3.d
Infinitive
Phrases**

An *infinitive phrase* contains the infinitive, its objects, and any modifiers. *See* **4.A.4.k**: Verbals.

to live near the ocean   to play happily   to try a new tactic

Infinitive phrases are used as nouns, adjectives, or adverbs.

I want *to go to the library*.
(The infinitive phrase is the object of the verb *want*.)

To become a pilot was his lifelong dream.
(The infinitive phrase is the predicate nominative.)

This is a meal *to savor slowly*.
(The infinitive phrase is an adjective that modifies the noun *meal*.)

I run every day *to stay in shape*.
(The infinitive phrase is an adverb that modifies the verb *run*.)

4.B.4
Clauses

A *clause* is a group of related words that contains both a subject and a predicate.

4.B.4.a
Independent Clauses

A clause that expresses a complete thought and can stand by itself is called an *independent clause* or a *main clause*. You can turn an independent clause into a simple sentence merely by adding a period.

The rooster crowed in the barn.
(The clause *the rooster crowed in the barn* is a complete thought and can stand by itself. Thus, it is an independent clause.)

An independent clause may be very long or very short.

Rain falls.

Roses are red.

Twenty people attended the ceremony.

The Spanish class visited a Mexican restaurant.

The man in the brown hat talking to the train conductor seems very angry about the delay.

4.B.4.b
Dependent Clauses

A clause that does not express a complete idea and cannot stand by itself is called a *dependent* or *subordinate clause*. A dependent clause depends upon the independent clause in the sentence to complete its meaning. Dependent clauses act as adjectives, adverbs, or nouns.

Adjective Clauses. Adjective clauses function in sentences exactly as single-word adjectives do. *See* **4.A.3**: Adjectives. They can modify any noun or pronoun in a sentence. They may be used in any of several ways.

To modify the subject:
The package *that Sue wrapped* was the prettiest.
(The adjective clause modifies *package*.)

To modify the predicate nominative:
The tall fire fighter is the one *who saved my cat*.
(The adjective clause modifies *one*.)

To modify the direct object:
The puppy chased the stick *that his master threw*.
(The adjective clause modifies *stick*.)

To modify an indirect object:
We sent our classmate *who was sick* a get-well card.
(The adjective clause modifies *classmate*.)

To modify the object of a preposition:
We walked up the hill *where the hut had been built*.
(The adjective clause modifies *hill*.)

Adverb Clauses. An adverb clause functions as an adverb. *See* **4.A.5**: Adverbs. Thus, it can modify any verb, adjective, or adverb in a sentence. It may be used in several ways.

To modify a verb:
We ate *when the guests had arrived*.
(The adverb clause modifies the verb *ate*.)

To modify an adjective:
I baked enough cupcakes *so that there is one for each child*.
(The adverb clause modifies the adjective *enough*.)

To modify an adverb:
The noise of the stereo was so loud *that I could not hear the phone*.
(The adverb clause modifies the adverb *so*.)

To modify a predicate adjective:
Rachel is often cranky *when she first wakes up*.
(The adverb clause modifies the predicate adjective *cranky*.)

Noun Clauses. A noun clause functions as a noun. *See* **4.A.1**: Nouns. It may be used in a sentence in any situation where a noun or pronoun may be used.

As a subject:
What happened at the party surprised everyone.
(The noun clause is the subject of the verb *surprised*.)

As a direct object:
Sarah knew *that her costume was attractive*.
(The noun clause acts as the object of the verb *knew*.)

As an indirect object:
We will give *whoever wants one* a copy of the entire speech.
(The noun clause acts as the indirect object of the verb *give*, answering the question, We will give the copy to whom?)

As the object of a preposition:
The campers took nothing except *what they could carry in their packs.*
(The noun clause acts as the object of the preposition *except.*)

As a predicate nominative:
The question is *whether we should build a house or buy one.*
(The noun clause is the predicate nominative after the linking verb *is.*)

As an appositive:
His first thought, *that the noise was a gunshot,* was incorrect.
(The noun clause acts as an appositive of the subject *thought.*)

By definition, a clause contains a subject and a predicate. Usually, both of these essential elements are expressed, leaving nothing to be understood. Sometimes, however, either the subject or the predicate is not expressed but is still understood to be part of the clause. When a clause has an essential element missing, it is called an *elliptical clause.*

4.B.4.c
Elliptical Clauses

Mrs. Jones retired in November; Mr. Jones retired a month later.
(two complete independent clauses)

Mrs. Jones retired in November; *Mr. Jones, a month later.*
(one complete independent clause followed by an elliptical independent clause in which the verb *retired* is understood)

While he was listening to the radio, Sam heard an interview with the senator.
(one complete dependent clause followed by one complete independent clause)

While listening to the radio, Sam heard an interview with the senator.
(one elliptical dependent clause, in which the subject *he* and the first word of the verb phrase *was listening* is understood, followed by one complete independent clause)

Elliptical clauses make sentences less wordy and add variety to passages that contain many sentences full of clauses.

Clauses can be either restrictive or nonrestrictive. A *restrictive clause* is a clause that is essential to the meaning of the sentence. That is, it restricts the meaning of the sentence by identifying a specific person or

4.B.4.d
Restrictive and Nonrestrictive Clauses

thing. A restrictive clause so limits or qualifies the word it modifies that it cannot be omitted without changing the meaning of the sentence. Restrictive clauses should be introduced with the relative pronoun *that, who,* or *whom* and should never be set off with commas.

A *nonrestrictive clause* is a clause that is not essential to the meaning of the sentence. It merely adds description to an already identified person or thing. A nonrestrictive clause can be omitted without changing the meaning of the sentence. Nonrestrictive clauses are introduced with *which, who,* or *whom.* They should always be enclosed by a pair of commas.

Restrictive: The crowd that was gathered in front of the stage was loud and unruly.

Nonrestrictive: The crowd, which had gathered in front of the stage to hear the concert, turned loud and unruly when the band failed to arrive.

Restrictive: The doctor who treated my sister had graduated from one of the best medical schools in the country.

Nonrestrictive: The doctor, who had graduated from one of the best medical schools in the country, was offered jobs at many excellent hospitals.

NOTE: A nonrestrictive clause, unless it begins or ends the sentence, should always be both preceded and followed by a comma. A common error is leaving out the second comma.

Incorrect: Nancy Payne, whom I knew in high school is now a stand-up comic.

Correct: Nancy Payne, whom I knew in high school, is now a stand-up comic.

Sometimes a sentence containing a relative clause is worded in such a way that only the punctuation makes it clear to readers whether the clause is restrictive or nonrestrictive. For this reason, it is important for you as a writer to be certain of the meaning you are trying to convey and of the correct punctuation for conveying it.

Nonrestrictive: In computer manuals, *which are badly written,* the explanations of functions are hard to understand. (This sentence suggests that all computer manuals are badly written.)

Restrictive: In computer manuals *that are badly written* the explanations of functions are hard to understand. (It's now clear that only some computer manuals are badly written and therefore hard to understand.)

Sentences may be classified in several ways. One useful form of classification is by structure. The four kinds of sentence structure are simple, compound, complex, and compound-complex.

4.C
Kinds of Sentences

Simple sentences are made up of one independent (main) clause and no dependent (subordinate) clauses. A simple sentence may contain a compound subject or a compound verb, or both a compound subject and a compound verb. In the following sentences, the subject is underlined once and the verb is underlined twice.

4.C.1
Simple Sentences

The boy ate the apple.

The windows are small.

A man and his son came to the store.
(compound subject)

The pianist bowed to the audience and sat down at the piano.
(compound verb)

My brother and sister love to swim and hate to ski.
(compound subject and compound verb)

Compound sentences contain two or more independent clauses and no dependent clauses. The clauses in a compound sentence are joined by coordinating conjunctions (*and, but, so,* and so forth), by conjunctive adverbs (*however, nevertheless,* and so forth), or simply by a semicolon. *See* **4.A.7**: Conjunctions *and* **4.A.5.a**: Types of Adverbs.

4.C.2
Compound Sentences

Carole made the lemonade and *Harry mixed the punch.*

We don't like horror movies; nevertheless, *we stayed to the end of the film.*

The guests have no way to get here; someone must pick them up.

111

4.C.3 Complex sentences

Complex sentences contain one independent clause and one or more dependent clauses.

```
  ┌─── dependent ───┐  ┌─── independent ───┐
Although Harry was late, we let him join the game.
```

```
  ┌─── dependent ───┐  ┌─ independent ─┐
After I finished my homework, I went to the store
```

```
  ┌─── dependent ───┐
that you told me about.
```

4.C.4 Compound-Complex Sentences

Compound-complex sentences contain two or more independent clauses and one or more dependent clauses.

```
  ┌─────── dependent ───────┐
When the house gets cold in the winter,
```

```
  ┌──── independent ────┐
Father lights a fire in the fireplace,
```

```
  ┌──── independent ────┐
and mother makes some hot chocolate.
```

```
  ┌─────── dependent ───────┐  ┌─ independent ─┐
If Sally can come to visit tomorrow, we'll go to the park;
```

```
┌─dependent─┐  ┌─── independent ───┐
if she can't,  I'll stay home and read.
```

4.C.5 What Sentences Do

Sentences may also be classified according to what they do and how ideas are presented in them. A sentence can state a fact or make an assertion, ask a question, give a command or make a request, or express strong feeling.

4.C.5.a Declarative Sentences

A sentence that states a fact or makes an assertion is a *declarative sentence*. Declarative sentences end with a period. Most of the sentences you write are declarative sentences.

The boy is tall.

The new factory provided jobs for many people in the community.

The tag at the back of Kim's blouse scratched her neck when she moved.

A sentence that asks a question is an *interrogative sentence*. Interrogative sentences end with a question mark.

4.C.5.b
Interrogative
Sentences

> Is there a shorter route to take to the mall?
> What time is it?
> Do you like Mexican food?

A sentence that gives a command or makes a request is an *imperative sentence*. *You* is the understood subject of imperative sentences. Commands may be followed by a period or an exclamation point; requests end with a period.

4.C.5.c
Imperative
Sentences

> Please take out the garbage.
> (request)
>
> Go away!
> (command)
>
> Bring the paper with you when you come in.
> (command)

A sentence that expresses strong feeling is an *exclamatory sentence*. Exclamatory sentences end with an exclamation point.

4.C.5.d
Exclamatory
Sentences

> You should be ashamed of yourself!
> I disagree completely!
> What a great idea!

Ideas may be arranged in sentences in a number of ways. For purposes of organization, sentences can be divided into loose, periodic, and balanced types.

4.C.6
**How Ideas
Are Arranged
in Sentences**

> **NOTE:** Good writing uses a combination of the different sentence types to add interest and rhythm. *See* **7.C.4**: Checking Writing Style.

Loose sentences present a complete idea first and then add details later to strengthen the statement.

4.C.6.a
Loose
Sentences

> The people gathered at the country house were all related by either blood, marriage, or adoption.
>
> The new team was a strong one, with a combination of enthusiastic rookies and seasoned athletes.

Loose sentences are direct and easy to follow, and they help the reader grasp the main idea quickly. However, too many loose sentences in succession can be boring.

**4.C.6.b
Periodic
Sentences**

Periodic sentences place the main thought or idea at the close of the sentence.

> If the bank is insured, depositors will be able to get their money back after a robbery.

> At the very end of his speech, Raymond Jackson announced that he had decided to run for Congress.

Periodic sentences can provide variety and often create a sense of drama by keeping the main idea until the end. When loose and periodic sentences are used together, writing gains added pace and interest.

**4.C.6.c
Balanced
Sentences**

Balanced sentences use the same or similar forms to present thoughts and ideas to be compared or contrasted.

> To write is difficult, to have written is joy.

> It is harder to watch defeat in silence than to experience defeat in action.

Balanced sentences have a definite beat. Used occasionally, they have a dramatic effect, but overuse may create a stiff and stilted tone.

Usage and Style

It's important to choose the right words and use them correctly if you want to convey your meaning clearly to your audience. This chapter will discuss word usage in both formal and informal situations. It will warn you about words, phrases, and constructions that are commonly misused and should be avoided. Proper forms of address also will be described.

5.A Correct Word Use

Some words and expressions that are acceptable in casual conversation are not acceptable in formal speaking or writing. Follow the standards of correct word use in all your formal speaking and writing—whether it be papers for school, or business letters and reports, or a speech to a group in your community. Using words and expressions correctly is a sign of a careful, thoughtful writer or speaker. *See* **5.C**: Bending the Rules *for advice on informal English.*

5.A.1 Usage Traps

Usage traps include using the wrong word for the situation or meaning intended and using an incorrect part of speech. The following list contains some of the most commonly misused words and expressions. Read through the list, then refer to it whenever you are in doubt about the correct use of a word or expression.

NOTE: For a more complete explanation of specific parts of speech, *See* **4.A**: Parts of Speech. For a list of additional words that may be confused, *see* **3.E**: Homophones.

a, an. *A* is used before words beginning with consonant *sounds*. *An* is used before words beginning with vowel *sounds* (regardless of what the initial letter is).

a table	*a* hat	*a* used car
an apple	*an* hour	*an* oven

aggravate, irritate. *Aggravate* means "to make an already troubled situation worse or more serious." *Irritate* means "to annoy, exasperate, or chafe."

Sitting in a draft *aggravated* my stiff neck.
Some detergents can *irritate* your skin.

agree to, agree with. You *agree* to a plan, but *agree with* another person.

all the farther, all the faster. Do not use these expressions when you mean *as far as* or *as fast as*.

although, though. *Although* usually introduces a clause that precedes the main clause. *Though* usually introduces one that follows.

Although many have succeeded, he failed completely, *though* he tried hard.

among, between. Use *among* to show the relation of more than two persons or things. Use *between* when dealing with two things (or more than two things if each is considered individually).

We are *among* friends.
I was standing *between* the sofa and the table.
The railroad runs *between* Chicago, Milwaukee, and Minneapolis.

amount, number. *Amount* is used with a unified bulk or lump sum. *Number* suggests separate, countable units.

The *amount* of money you have depends on the *number* of coins and dollars.

and etc. Do not use this expression. Because *etc.* already means "and so forth," adding *and* is redundant.

anticipate, expect. Use *anticipate* when you mean "to prepare for something." Use *expect* when you mean "to think something will occur."

They *anticipated* the storm by going to a safe place.
We *expect* the mail will be delayed.

anxious, eager. *Anxious* suggests anxiety or worry. *Eager* means "looking forward to or wanting to."

We are *anxious* about the safety of the hostages.
I am *eager* to start my vacation.

anyplace, anywhere. Use *anywhere*. This holds true for *everywhere, nowhere,* and *somewhere*.

anyways, anywheres. These are not acceptable in formal writing. Use *anyway* and *anywhere*.

apt, liable, likely. *Apt* suggests fitness or suitability. *Liable* suggests obligation. *Likely* indicates probability.

She is an *apt* musician.
They were held *liable* for damages.
The rain is *likely* to arrive here this evening.

bad, badly. *Bad* is an adjective. *Badly,* an adverb. Use *bad* after linking verbs (*is, feels, tastes*).

He was a *bad* boy today.
The engine misfired *badly*.
She feels *bad* about missing the concert.

bring, take. *Bring* indicates motion toward a speaker. *Take* indicates motion away.

Bring me the soup and *take* the plates from the table.

bursted, bust, busted. Never use *bursted*. The past tense of *burst* is *burst*. *Bust* and *busted* are slang uses of *burst*; they should not be used in formal writing.

The pipe *burst* today.   The pipe *is bursting* now.
The pipe *burst* yesterday.   This pipe *has burst* before.

can, may. *Can* means "is able to." *May* means "has permission to."

You *can* sketch well when you take your time.
After you have put everything away, you *may* leave.

compare, contrast. *Compare* is commonly used in two senses: to point out likenesses (*compare to*) and to examine two or more objects to find both likenesses and differences (*compare with*). *Contrast* means "to point out differences."

compare to, compare with. *Compare to* means "to point out general or metaphorical resemblances." *Compare with* means "to note specific similarities or differences between persons or things of the same kind."

He *compared* the sea *to* a woman, and his paintings of waves were tranquil *compared with* those of Jones.

data. *Data* is the plural form of the Latin word *datum*. It can be used as a collective singular noun when referring to a body of information as a unit.

The *data* (information) was available to everyone.
The *data* (figures) in this chart are confusing.

different than, different from. The preferred use is *different from*.

Rich people are *different from* you and me.

disinterested, uninterested. *Disinterested* means "unbiased." *Uninterested* means "having no interest in."

The dispute was settled by a *disinterested* party.
I am *uninterested* in your dispute.

doubt but, help but. Do not use these expressions in formal writing.

due to, because of. Do not use *due to* for *because of, owing to,* or *on account of. Due to* is correct after a linking verb, or as an adjective following a noun.

Incorrect: *Due to* heavy traffic, I was late.
Correct: *Because of* heavy traffic, I was late.
             My tardiness was *due to* heavy traffic.

each . . . are. *Each* implies "one" and takes a singular verb. Plural words used in phrases that modify *each* do not change the number of the verb.

Each woman *was* promoted.
Each of the women *was* promoted.

ecology, environment. *Ecology* is the study of the relationship of living things to each other and their *environment* (surrounding conditions).

Pollution affects the *environment*; *ecology* attempts to determine how.

either means "one or the other," not "both." *Either* is followed by *or,* not *nor.*

Do not say, "There are lions behind *either* door" when there are lions behind *both* doors.

enthuse. Do not use the verb *enthuse* in formal writing. Use *showed enthusiasm* or *was enthusiastic.*

Incorrect: He *enthused* about the new project.
Correct: He *showed enthusiasm* about the new project.
       He *was enthusiastic* about the new project.

etc. Avoid using this expression in formal writing. Instead, use *and so forth, and the like,* or a similar phrase. Or say specifically what you mean.

Incorrect: Use books, magazines, *etc.,* to do your research.
Correct: Use books, magazines, *and the like* to do your research.
       Use books, magazines, *and other library materials* to do your research.

fewer, less. *Fewer* applies to things that can be numbered or counted. *Less* applies to things in bulk, in the abstract, or in degree and value.

There are *fewer* houses here because there is *less* land.

fish, fishes. *Fish* is the plural for many of one kind, but *fishes* is used to refer to different species.

Halibut, mackerel, and salmon are the most abundant *fishes* in those waters.

fulsome means "disgusting or offensive to good taste, especially as being overdone," not "ample or abundant."

good, well. *Good* is an adjective; *well,* an adverb. *Well* acts as an adjective only when describing someone's health.

I had a *good* time; the dinner had been planned *well.*

She felt *good* about the project, but she did not feel *well* enough to go to work.

had best, had better, had ought. Use *ought to* or *should.*

hanged, hung. Criminals are *hanged*; things (pictures, clothes, drapes) are *hung.*

hardly, scarcely. *Hardly* means "done with difficulty" or "barely able to." *Scarcely* refers to an insufficient quantity.

> I could *hardly* push the power mower; I had *scarcely* any energy left.

have got. Use just *have*.

> **Incorrect:** I've got it.
> **Correct:**   I have it.

imply, infer. *Imply* means "to suggest or hint at." *Infer* means "to draw a conclusion."

> He *implied* that the company was not doing well.
>
> After reading the article, I *inferred* that the country is in a recession.

in, into. *In* suggests being inside. *Into* suggests the act of entering.

> When I walked *into* the room, she was sitting *in* my chair.

inside of, off of, outside of. When used in prepositional phrases, the word *of* is not necessary.

> I keep my wallet *inside* my purse.
> He stood *outside* the door.

irregardless, disregardless. Do not use either of these words; they constitute double negatives. Use *regardless*.

is when, is where. Do not use these phrases when writing definitions or explanations.

> **Incorrect:** Writing *is when* you put your thoughts on paper.
> **Correct:**   Writing *is* putting your thoughts on paper.
>
> **Incorrect:** A trilogy *is where* there are three related books.
> **Correct:**   A trilogy is a series of three related books.

its, it's. *Its* is the possessive of *it*. *It's* is the contraction for *it is*.

> *It's* sad that the dog broke *its* foot.

kind, sort, type. These are singular nouns and must be modified by singular adjectives.

> *this kind* but *these kinds*
> *this type* but *those types*

kind of a, sort of a, type of a. The word *a* is incorrect. Also, do not use *kind of, sort of,* or *type of* in place of *somewhat, rather,* or *almost.*

What *kind of* material are you using?
I'm *somewhat* undecided.

leave, let. *Leave* means "to depart" or "to allow to remain in a certain condition." *Let* means "to allow, enable, or not interfere with."

I will *leave* the room and *let* you come in.
Leave the window open.

lie, lay. *Lie* means "to recline." The principal parts of the verb *lie* are *lie, lay, lain, lying. Lay* means "to put or place." The principal parts of *lay* are *lay, laid, laying.*

Lie down and rest.
I *lay down* yesterday to rest.
I *had lain* down to rest.
I *was lying* on the couch.

Will you *lay* the tile?
I *laid* the tile yesterday.
I *have laid* tile before.
We *are laying* the tile.

like, as. *As* is a conjunction; use *as* to join clauses. *Like* is a preposition; *like* plus a noun or pronoun forms a prepositional phrase.

I did the assignment *as* I was instructed to do it.
My sister looks *like* me. I look *like* Aunt Ruth.

loan, lend. *Loan* is a noun. *Lend* is a verb.

I will *lend* you the money, but this *loan* must be paid in full.

lots, lots of, a whole lot. Use *many, much,* or *a great deal* in place of these expressions.

Incorrect: Sean has *lots of* friends.
Correct: Sean has *many* friends.

median, mean, average. *Median* refers to the middle. *Mean* and *average* refer to the total of all components divided by the number of components. *Average* refers to the quantity involved, not to the person.

The *median* income of Moeburg is $22,500; its *mean* summer temperature is 72°F.

Incorrect: The *average* American eats 8 pounds of cheese annually.
Correct: Americans eat an *average* of 8 pounds of cheese per person annually.

neither should be followed by *nor,* not *or.*

> *Neither* the teacher *nor* the students knew where to board the train.

of. *Of* should never be used in place of *have* after auxiliary verbs.

> **Incorrect:** I could *of* danced all night.
> **Correct:** I could *have* danced all night.

over, more than. *Over* refers to relationships in space. *More than* is used with numbers.

> The airplane flew *over* a city with a population of *more than* 500,000.

pair, pairs. *Pair* is singular but can be used as a plural after a numeral or an adjective of number such as *several.*

> She bought a *pair* of gloves and six *pairs* (or *pair*) of socks.

preceding, previous. *Preceding* means "to come before." *Previous* means "to come before at other times."

> In 1985, we made more money than in the *preceding* year but not as much as in *previous* years.

raise, rise. *Raise* is a transitive verb requiring an object. Its principal parts are *raise, raised, raised, raising. Rise,* an intransitive verb, does not require an object. Its principal parts are *rise, rose, risen, rising.*

> I *raised* tomatoes and corn.
> Please *rise* when the judge enters.

real, really. *Real* is an adjective meaning "genuine or having reality." *Really* is an adverb meaning "actually or truly."

> The stone looked like a *real* diamond, but it *really* was a fake.

reason is because. Do not use this construction. Instead, say, *reason is* or *reason is that.*

> **Incorrect:** The *reason* I am late *is because* the car stalled.
> **Correct:** The *reason* I am late *is that* the car stalled.

seen, saw. The principal parts of *see* are *see, saw, seen, seeing.*

Incorrect:	I *seen* them at the store.
	We *have saw* the movie.
Correct:	I *saw* them at the store.
	We *have seen* the movie.

shall, will. Use *shall* with *I* and *we* in the future tense and in legal papers and directives. Use *will* with *he, she, it,* and *they* and with *I* and *we* when expressing a promise.

I *shall* go to work; she *will* go to school.
The buyer *shall* have clear title to the property.
I *will* do all that I can to help you.

sit, set. *Sit* means "to place oneself." *Set* means "to put or place something."

Sit down and rest awhile. I will *set* the box on the floor.

so. Do not use *so* in place of *so that, therefore,* or *thus.* Do not use *so* to mean "very" in formal writing (*so* kind).

such as, like. Use *such as* for examples. Use *like* for resemblances.

Some ships, *such as* ocean liners, are *like* small cities.

temperatures get higher or lower, not warmer or cooler.

that, which. *That* is used chiefly to begin restrictive clauses (clauses that are essential to the meaning of the sentence). *Which* is used to begin nonrestrictive clauses (clauses that are not essential, but simply provide additional information).

| **Restrictive:** | The house *that* I liked was not for sale. |
| **Nonrestrictive:** | My house, *which* is old, needs many repairs. |

then, also. These words are adverbs. Do not use them instead of conjunctions.

Incorrect:	He ate breakfast, *then* went to work.
	We enjoy skiing, *also* skating.
Correct:	He ate breakfast *and* then went to work.
	We enjoy skiing *and* skating.

there, their, they're. *There* means "in or at that place." *Their* is a possessive pronoun. *They're* is a contraction for *they are.*

I parked the car *there*.
Their house was custom-built.
They're going to leave soon.

try and. Do not use *try and* in formal writing. Use *try to*.

Incorrect: I will *try and* finish the painting today.
Correct: I will *try to* finish the painting today.

type. Do not use as a substitute for *type of*.

Incorrect: I would like to buy this *type* dress.
Correct: I would like to buy this *type of* dress.

unique. *Unique* means "the only one of its kind" or "without equal." Do not use *more, most,* or *very* with *unique*.

very. *Very* is an overused adverb. Try to use more specific modifiers, or use words that are strong in themselves. This same advice applies to *so, surely, too, extremely, indeed.*

Weak: She sings *very* well.
Improved: She sings *beautifully*.
She is a *talented* singer.

were, was. *Were* is used when a statement is contrary to fact, expresses a wish, or states a doubtful situation. *Was* is used for statements of fact in the past.

If he *were* here, he would be as wise as he *was* during the war.

while. *While* means "during the time that." Do not use *while* in place of *although, and, but,* or *whereas*.

Incorrect: The days were hot, *while* the nights were cool.
Correct: The days were hot, *but* the nights were cool.
The days were hot *while* we were on vacation.

who, whom. Use *who* as a subject. Use *whom* as an object.

That is the boy *who* threw the rock.
(*who* is the subject of *threw*)

The girl for *whom* I bought the gift was delighted.
(*whom* is the object of the preposition *for*)

My mother, *who* is often late, came early.
(*who* is the subject of *is*)

In English, there are many words that sound or look similar but have different meanings. Such words often lead to errors in usage or spelling.

ability, capability. *Ability* is the skill to perform. *Capability* is the ability of a person to learn or to do something or the ability of a thing to do something.

> The captain has the *ability* to steer the ship, which has a *capability* of thirty knots.

accept, except. *Accept* means "to receive willingly." *Except* means "to exclude." As a preposition, *except* means "other than."

> I will *accept* the first part of your proposal, but I must *except* the second part.
>
> I jog every day *except* Sunday.

adapt, adept, adopt. *Adapt* means "to make suitable." *Adept,* "to be skilled or expert." *Adopt,* "to take for one's own."

adjoin, adjourn. *Adjoin* means "to be next to." *Adjourn* means "to put off until later."

advice, advise. *Advice* is a noun. *Advise,* a verb. Do not use *advise* to mean "inform" or "tell." Save it for "give notice" or "warn."

> She gave me good *advice* when she *advised* me not to hitchhike.

affect, effect. *Affect* is a verb meaning "to influence." *Effect,* as a verb, means "to cause, bring about, or accomplish"; as a noun, *effect* means "a result or an accomplishment."

> His presence *affected* the mood of the party.
> A treaty was *effected* after many months of meetings.
> The symphony had a wonderful *effect* on the audience.

allay, ally. *Allay* means "to put at rest." *Ally* means "to unite."

> The countries *allied* (became *allies*) to *allay* the possibility of attack.

all right, alright. *All right* is always completely right, but *alright* should not be used.

all together, altogether. *All together* means "everyone in a group." *Altogether* means "completely or entirely."

Altogether there are nine people when the group is *all together*.

allude, elude. *Allude* means "to make an indirect reference to something." *Elude* means "to avoid or evade." Don't confuse *allude* with *refer,* "to make a direct reference to a specific thing."

He *alluded* to a time in the past when he was happy.
The instructor *referred* us to page 20 in the text.
The refugees *eluded* the border patrol.

allusion, illusion. You make an *allusion* by referring indirectly to a person or thing, while an *illusion* is an unreal or misleading appearance.

amiable, amicable. *Amiable* describes a friendly, good natured person. *Amicable* describes a peaceful, friendly relationship.

ante, anti. *Ante* means "before"; *anti* means "against."

appraise, apprise. *Appraise* means "to estimate value." *Apprise* means "to inform."

He *appraised* the vase, then *apprised* the owner of its value.

arms, alms. *Arms* refers to part of the body or weapons. *Alms* refers to gifts to the poor.

as large as, larger than. *As large as* is used when you want to say that something is two or more times bigger than something else. *Larger than* compares two things.

Colorado is three times *as large as* Maine, but Texas is *larger than* Colorado.

assay, essay. An *assay* is an analysis of an item's components. An *essay* is a written composition.

He wrote an *essay* on how to *assay* gold ore.

averse, adverse. *Averse* means "opposed to or repelled by." *Adverse* means "bad or unfavorable."

You are probably *averse* to *adverse* weather.

awhile, a while. *Awhile* is an adverb. *While* (as in *a while*) is a noun. Use *a while* after prepositions (for *a while,* after *a while*).

Work *awhile* longer, and I'll help you.
She stood there for *a while*.

bases, basis. *Bases* are underlying supports or a series of stations. *Basis* means "the foundation or principal component."

The *bases* were built on the *basis* of a survey.

beau, bough, bow. *Beau* means "suitor." *Bough* means "main branch of a tree." Depending on pronunciation, *bow* means either "to incline the body in salute"or "a knotted ribbon."

She fixed the *bow* in her hair and acknowledged the *bow* of her *beau* when they met under the maple *bough*.

beside, besides. *Beside* means "alongside of." *Besides* means "in addition to."

He sat *beside* me.
Besides the mortgage, I have car payments to make.

biannual, biennial. *Biannual* means "twice a year." *Biennial* means "once every two years."

capital, capitol. Use *capital* (with an *a*) when referring to money, upper-case letters, a city in which a government is located, or crimes punishable by death. Use *capitol* (with an *o*) only when referring to a building where legislatures meet.

Capitol has a *capital C* if it means the building in which the Congress of the United States meets.

casual, causal. *Casual* means "happening by chance" or "informal in manner." *Causal* refers to the cause of (something).

censor, censure. As a verb, censor means "to act as a censor." *Censure* means "to blame or criticize."

She *censured* him for *censoring* the letter.

charted, charter. *Charted* involves maps. A *charter* is a written grant or order.

clench, clinch. *Clench* means "to close tightly." *Clinch* means "to fasten or settle decisively."

She *clenched* her teeth as she *clinched* the deal.

click, clique. *Click* is a sound. A *clique* is a group of people.

climactic, climatic. *Climactic* refers to a climax. *Climatic* refers to the climate.

complement, compliment. A *complement* is something that completes or goes with an item. A *compliment* refers to praise.

confidant, confident. A *confidant* is a trusted person. One who is *confident* holds a firm belief.

continual, continuous. *Continual* implies a recurrence at frequent intervals. *Continuous* means "extending uninterruptedly."

The *continual* hammering gave him a *continuous* headache.

credible, creditable, credulous. *Credible* means "believable." *Creditable* means "worthy of esteem or praise." *Credulous* means "gullible."

His account of the situation was *credible*.
He made a *creditable* contribution to the project.
Credulous people believe everything that they are told.

decree, degree. *Decree* is something ordered by authority, while *degree* is a stage in a process or an academic award.

defer, differ. *Defer* means "to put off or yield." *Differ* means "to be unlike or disagree."

descent, dissent. *Descent* refers to coming or going down. *Dissent* means "to disagree."

desert, dessert. Do not confuse *desert* (a place of little rainfall) with *dessert* (sweets or the like served at the end of a meal).

desolate, dissolute. A desert is *desolate* (barren). People who have no morals are *dissolute*.

disburse, disperse. You *disburse* (pay out) money, but you *disperse* (distribute) handbills.

discomfit, discomfort. *Discomfit* means "to overthrow, defeat, or embarrass." *Discomfort* refers to uneasiness.

distract, detract. *Distract* means "to draw away or confuse." *Detract* means "to take away from."

The defect *distracts* your attention and *detracts* from the value.

elicit, illicit. *Elicit* is a verb meaning "to draw out something that is hidden or held back." *Illicit* is an adjective meaning "unlawful or improper."

The police *elicited* from him the hiding place of the *illicit* drug.

emigrate, immigrate. *Emigrate* means "to move out of a country." *Immigrate*, "to move into a country."

They *emigrated* from Ireland. She *immigrated* to Canada.

eminent, imminent. Do not say someone is *eminent* (distinguished) when you mean his or her arrival is *imminent* (about to occur).

ensure, insure. Both words mean "to make certain," but *insure* usually is confined to the meaning "guarantee against loss."

His house was *insured* against fire to *ensure* that he would have money to buy another if it burned down.

envelop, envelope. *Envelop* is a verb meaning "to wrap or cover." *Envelope* is a noun referring to stationery or an enclosing covering.

equable, equitable. *Equable* means "uniform." *Equitable* means "fair."

Equable distribution is the only *equitable* way.

errand, errant. Do not refer to an *errand* (a short trip, or the purpose of the trip) as an *errant*, which means "wandering or incorrect."

exalt, exult. *Exalt* means "to raise in rank or to fill with pride." *Exult* means "to rejoice."

extant, extent. *Extant* means "still existing." *Extent* means "the amount to which something extends."

This *extant* animal roams the range's whole *extent*.

farther, further. Use *farther* to suggest a measurable distance. Use *further* to show a greater degree, extent, quantity, or time. *Further* also means "moreover" and "in addition to."

We walked *farther* than we had to.
We can discuss this matter *further* tomorrow.

flounder, founder. As a verb, *flounder* means "to struggle." *Founder* means "to stumble or sink" or "the person who establishes something."

They *floundered* for life jackets as the boat began to *founder*.

flout, flaunt. *Flout* means "treat with contempt." *Flaunt* means "display boldly."

They *flout* their work and *flaunt* their clothes.

fondling, foundling. *Fondling* refers to treating lovingly. *Foundling* is a noun meaning "a deserted child."

formally, formerly. *Formally* means "in a formal manner." *Formerly* means "in the past."

Jan Smith, *formerly* of Jones, Brown, and Little, was *formally* attired for the opening of Smith, Green, and Wilson.

gamut, gauntlet. *Gamut* refers to the whole range of something. *Gauntlet* is a method of punishment or a glove.

hallow, hollow. *Hallow* means "holy or sacred." *Hollow* means "empty inside."

hospitable, hospital. *Hospitable* refers to friendly treatment. A *hospital* is a place for sick or injured persons.

incite, insight. Do not confuse *incite* (the act of stirring up) with *insight* (understanding or wisdom).

incredible, incredulous. *Incredible* means "unbelievable." *Incredulous* means "unbelieving."

They felt *incredulous* about his *incredible* story.

inequity, iniquity. *Inequity* refers to unfairness. *Iniquity* refers to wickedness.

ingenious, ingenuous. *Ingenious* means "clever or skillful." *Ingenuous* means "frank, simple, sincere."

insolate, insulate. *Insolate* means "to expose to the sun." *Insulate* means "to keep from losing heat or cold, or to set apart."

intense, intents. *Intense* means "very strong." *Intents* means "purposes."

She felt *intense* about her career *intents*.

interment, internment. Do not confuse *interment* (burial) and *internment* (confinement).

interstate, intrastate, intestate. *Interstate* means "between states." *Intrastate* means "within a state." *Intestate* means "without a will."

key, quay, cay. *Key* refers to a locking device. *Key* and *cay* both refer to a low island or reef. *Quay* is a landing place for ships.

later, latter. *Later* means "more late." *Latter* means "the second of two."

John and Joe were both *late*, but the *latter* was *later*.

lesser, lessor. *Lesser* means "the less important of two." A *lessor* is a person who grants a lease.

liable, libel. *Liable* means "likely or bound by law." *Libel* refers to a false or damaging statement.

loath, loathe. *Loath* is an adjective that means "unwilling." *Loathe* is a verb that means "to feel a strong dislike."

I am *loath* to take the subway, but I *loathe* looking for a parking place.

lose, loose. *Lose* means "to stop having." *Loose* (verb) means "to set free," or (adjective) "not fastened."

moral, morale. Do not write *moral* (concerning right conduct) when you mean *morale* (mental condition as regards courage and confidence).

ordinance, ordnance. Do not confuse *ordinance* (a rule or law) with *ordnance* (military weapons).

perform, preform. *Perform* means "to carry out or to give a performance." *Preform* means "to form or shape beforehand."

The orchestra *performed* beautifully.
The patio is made of *preformed* concrete.

personal, personnel. *Personal* has to do with a person's private affairs. *Personnel* refers to people employed in an organization.

practicable, practical. *Practicable* means "capable of being put into practice." *Practical* means "being useful or successful."

The proposed plan seemed *practicable*.
She always finds *practical* solutions for our problems.

prescribe, proscribe. You *prescribe* when you order or direct something. You *proscribe* when you prohibit or condemn something.

pretext, pretense. A *pretext* is put forward to conceal a truth. A *pretense* is intended to conceal personal feelings.

principal, principle. *Principal* as a noun refers to a sum of money or to a person or thing of first importance; as an adjective, *principal* means "first, chief, or main." *Principle* is a noun meaning "a law, code, doctrine, or rule."

> The *principal* of the loan was $70,000.
> Our *principal* is Ms. Smith.
> She is a woman of high *principles*.

reluctant, reticent. If you do not want to act, you are *reluctant*. If you do not want to speak, you are *reticent*.

respectfully, respectively. *Respectfully* means "in a respectful manner." *Respectively* means "each in the order given."

> I am *respectfully* submitting this report for your approval.
> In the 1930's, Naziism and Fascism were political movements in Germany and Italy, *respectively*.

speciality, specialty. *Speciality* means "the special character of something." *Specialty* refers to a special line of work or business.

> American history is the *speciality* of that college, and his *specialty* is the Civil War period.

species, specie. *Species* refers to a kind or class. *Specie* refers to money in the form of coin.

tenant, tenet. A *tenant* is an occupant or renter. A *tenet* is a doctrine or belief.

then, than. Use *than* in comparisons. Use *then* when time is involved or you mean *also*.

> This train is faster *than* that one, but *then* it has a more powerful locomotive.

to, too, two. *To* is a preposition (*to* the store) and the sign of an infinitive (*to* walk). *Too* is an adverb meaning "also" or "more than what is proper or enough." *Two* is the number (*two* cats).

tortuous, torturous. *Tortuous* means "full of twists and turns." *Torturous* refers to inflicting pain.

> The sun was *torturous* as he rode through the *tortuous* ravines.

track, tract. *Track* refers to a path or a sport. *Tract* refers to a stretch of land or water.

waive, wave. *Waive* refers to giving something up. *Wave* refers to movements like the surge or swell of water.

weather, whether. You should not confuse *weather* (the condition of the atmosphere) with *whether,* an expression of choice or alternative.

wet, whet. *Wet* is the opposite of dry. *Whet* means "to sharpen by rubbing or to make keen."

whither, wither. Use *whither* to mean "to what place." *Wither* means "a loss of freshness or vigor."

In addition to the misuse of words and phrases, writing can suffer from the misuse of grammatical constructions. Common problems in this area include errors in agreement, faulty pronoun references, shifts in point of view, words used as the wrong parts of speech, fragmentary or run-on sentences, split constructions, nonparallel constructions, and problems with modifiers.

These errors confuse readers by hiding the writer's thoughts. Worse, they can completely change the writer's meaning. This section explains how to avoid the most serious problems in grammatical constructions. *See also* **4.A**: Parts of Speech *and* **4.B**: Parts of a Sentence.

5.B
Misused Constructions

Agreement can be an issue with either subjects and verbs or pronouns and their verbs and antecedents.

5.B.1
Agreement Problems

A verb must agree with its subject in number and person.

5.B.1.a
Subject-Verb Agreement

Number: The *paper was* at the door.
(singular)

The *papers were* on my desk.
(plural)

Person: Singular	**Plural**
I am at home.	*We are* at home.
You are at home.	*You are* at home.
He, she, it is at home.	*They are* at home.

Following are some additional reminders about subject-verb agreement.

1. When other parts of a sentence come between the subject and the verb, these parts do not change the person or the number of the verb.

    The *boys* who had a good time at the party *are* now playing softball.

    The *report* about leases and contracts *was* distributed.

2. Inverting the order of the subject and verb does not affect agreement.

    In the trunk *were piles* of money.
    (*Piles were . . . .*)

3. Some nouns are plural in form but are singular in meaning and therefore take singular verbs.

    The *news was* bad.
    The *United Nations is* located in New York.
    Measles *has been* all too common this year.

    Some nouns are plural in form but may be either singular or plural, depending on their meaning in the sentence. Among these nouns are *economics, athletics, politics, ethics.*

    Politics is the art of the possible.
    His *politics are* constantly changing.

4. Two or more subjects joined by *and* take a plural verb.

    The *baby and* the *dog love* attention.
    (*They love . . . .*)

    If the two subjects form a single idea or are thought of as a unit, they should take a singular verb.

    Macaroni and cheese is my favorite dish.
    (*It* is . . . .)

5. Singular subjects joined by *or* or *nor* take a singular verb.

    Either the *house or* the *garage is* on fire.

    If the subjects joined by *or* or *nor* differ in number or person, the verb agrees with the subject nearer the verb.

Neither the *lamp nor* the *bulbs were* working.
Either the *trees or* the *lawn needs* cutting.

6. A collective noun takes a singular verb when the group is regarded as a unit. But a collective noun takes a plural verb when emphasis is placed on the individual members of the group.

The *audience was* applauding.
(*applauding* together)

The *audience were* arriving.
(*arriving* separately)

Pronouns used as subjects must agree with their verbs and with their antecedents. Following are some rules for making pronouns agree with their verbs and their antecedents.

1. When using indefinite pronouns as subjects, be careful to choose the correct form of the verb.

These indefinite pronouns are considered to be singular and take singular verbs: *each, either, neither,* and all pronouns ending in *-body* or *-one.*

Everyone is here.
Nobody wants to be sick.
Each of these apples *is* spoiled.

These indefinite pronouns are considered to be plural and take plural verbs: *both, few, many, several.*

Both of you *are* going to succeed.
Many are called, but *few are* chosen.

All, any, most, none, and *some* may be either singular or plural, depending on their meaning in the sentence. When the pronoun refers to one thing or to a quantity as a whole, use a singular verb. When the pronoun refers to a number of individual items, use a plural verb.

Some of the money *was* missing.
(singular)

Some of their friends *were* there.
(plural)

All of my hope *is* gone.
(singular)

All of you *are* invited.
(plural)

135

2. When the subject is a relative pronoun (*who, which, that*), the verb should agree with the pronoun's antecedent.

   She is the editor *who speaks* Spanish.
   (editor speaks)

   The dogs *that were barking* are quiet now.
   (dogs were barking)

3. A pronoun agrees with its antecedent in gender, number, and person.

   The *woman* picked up *her* briefcase.
   The *women* picked up *their* briefcases.

   Be especially careful when the pronoun's antecedent is an indefinite pronoun. Follow the preceding rules for deciding if the indefinite pronoun is singular or plural. Then make the other pronoun agree with the indefinite pronoun.

   Neither of the girls is wearing *her* coat.
   All of the girls are wearing *their* coats.

4. When the antecedent is a collective noun, the pronoun is either singular or plural—depending on whether the collective noun is singular or plural in the sentence.

   The *board* made *its* decision.
   The *board* discussed the matter among *themselves*.

5.B.2 Faulty Pronoun References

Every pronoun must have an antecedent. Place each pronoun as close as possible to its antecedent so that it is clear what word the pronoun refers back to.

1. Avoid confusing references. A reader will be confused if a sentence contains two possible antecedents for a pronoun.

   Confusing: After Michael talked to Bill, he was angry.

   Clearer: After Michael talked to Bill, Bill was angry.
   or Michael was angry after he talked to Bill.

2. Avoid vague references, which occur when the antecedent of a pronoun is not actually stated.

Using *they, this, that,* and *which* to refer to an entire statement (rather than to one noun) is a common form of vague reference.

Vague: I had not finished the report, *which* irritated Mr. Brown.

Clearer: The fact that I had not finished the report irritated Mr. Brown. *or*
My failure to finish the report irritated Mr. Brown.

3.   Avoid the indefinite use of *it, they,* and *you.*

Confusing: In the first act, *it* shows Hamlet's character.

Clearer: In the first act, Hamlet's character is shown. *or*
In the first act, Hamlet shows his character.

Your writing should be as consistent as possible. Shifts in approach include changes in number, subject, tense, and voice. Of course, there are times when you do need to change your approach. But frequent and unnecessary shifts are confusing.

**5.B.3
Shifts in
Approach**

1.   Avoid unnecessary shifts in number (singular and plural).

Incorrect: *Plants are* decorative, but *it requires* much care.
Correct: *Plants are* decorative, but *they require* much care.

2.   Avoid unnecessary shifts in the subjects in sentences.

Incorrect: If *you* do your research, *it* will be a good paper.
Correct: If *you* do your research, *you* will write a good paper.

3.   Avoid unnecessary shifts in tense (present, past, future).

Incorrect: Jack *came* home and *took* off his jacket. He *walks* to his room and *changes* clothes. Ten minutes later, he *was* ready to eat dinner.
Correct: Jack *came* home and *took* off his jacket. He *walked* to his room and *changed* clothes. Ten minutes later, he *was* ready to eat dinner.

4.   Avoid unnecessary shifts in voice (active and passive).

Incorrect: He *did* good work, but no raise *was received.*
Correct: He *did* good work, but he *received* no raise.

5.B.4
Sentence
Faults

Sentence faults occur when you write sentences that are incomplete or when you improperly run sentences together. To review basic sentence structure, *see* **4.B**: Parts of a Sentence.

5.B.4.a
Sentence
Fragments

A *sentence fragment* is an incomplete sentence. If you put a period at the end of a phrase or a subordinate clause, you will have a fragment. Phrases and subordinate clauses cannot stand alone. *See also* **5.C.4.h**: Sentence Fragments *for an exception to this rule.*

You can correct a sentence fragment by joining it to a sentence.

Fragment: *After going to college for four years.* I was ready to teach.
Correct: After going to college for four years, I was ready to teach.

Fragment: *Although I awoke earlier than usual.* I was late for work.
Correct: Although I awoke earlier than usual, I was late for work.

Sometimes you can add words or change the wording to make the fragment a complete sentence in itself.

Fragment: Watching the election results all night.
Correct: *I was* watching the election results all night.

Fragment: One of my friends *who* lost her ring in the swimming pool.
Correct: One of my friends lost her ring in the swimming pool.

5.B.4.b
Run-On
Sentences

A *run-on sentence* is two or more sentences improperly joined together. A comma alone cannot properly join sentences together. The following are run-on sentences because only a comma appears between the two clauses.

Run-on: The managers from the New York office toured the plant, they made a favorable report.

Run-on: The board is scheduled to meet tomorrow, it has many matters to discuss.

Run-on: Classes started on September 5, however, I did not register until September 7.

Run-on sentences can be corrected in several ways.

1. Make two separate sentences.

The managers from the New York office toured the plant. They made a favorable report.

2. Use a semicolon between the clauses.

Classes started on September 5; however, I did not register until September 7.

3. Use a comma and a conjunction between the clauses (such as *and, but, or,* or *nor*).

The managers from the New York office toured the plant, *and* they made a favorable report.

4. Make one of the statements into a phrase or a subordinate clause.

Scheduled to meet tomorrow, the board has many matters to discuss.

Another error is to run sentences together with no punctuation at all between them. These run-together sentences must also be separated or properly connected.

Run-on: I spent $54 for this dress I like the style.

Correct: I spent $54 for this dress. I like the style.
I spent $54 for this dress because I like the style.
I spent $54 for this dress; I like the style.

Run-on: Why are you leaving now wait I'll walk home with you.

Correct: Why are you leaving now? Wait! I'll walk home with you.
Why are you leaving now? Wait and I'll walk home with you.

5.B.5
Split
Constructions

Sometimes writers unnecessarily split infinitives, separate subjects from verbs, or separate parts of a verb phrase. When writers do any of these things, they are splitting constructions. The following list contains examples of split constructions to avoid.

1. Avoid split infinitives. An infinitive is *to* plus a verb (*to walk, to think*). *See also* **5.C.4.b**: Split Infinitives *for an exception to this rule.* Putting other words between *to* and the verb is often awkward.

   Awkward: To be or *to* not *be*: that is the question.
   Better: To be or not *to be*: that is the question.

   Awkward: We had *to* without any preparation or warning *pack* our belongings.
   Better: We had *to pack* our belongings without any preparation or warning.

2. Avoid unnecessarily separating a subject and its verb or a verb and its object. Keeping these basic sentence parts together usually makes your writing clearer.

   Awkward: *Mary,* in one bounding leap, *cleared* the fence. (subject and verb separated)
   Awkward: Mary *cleared,* in one bounding leap, *the fence.* (verb and object separated)
   Better: *Mary cleared the fence* in one bounding leap.

3. Do not separate a preposition from its object.

   Awkward: He walked *into,* since he was in the neighborhood, *the museum.*
   Better: Since he was in the neighborhood, he walked *into the museum.*

4. Do not separate the parts of a verb phrase.

   Awkward: Mary *has,* although you would not think so, *been* ill.
   Better: Mary *has been* ill, although you would not think so.

   Awkward: I *might have,* if you had not opposed me, *bought* the stocks.
   Better: If you had not opposed me, I *might have bought* the stocks.

Parallel construction involves expressing two or more related ideas in the same grammatical form. To make a pair of ideas parallel, state both ideas in the same structure—in the same kind of words, phrases, or clauses. You should also use parallel structure in a series of items joined by *and* or *or*. Following are some examples of parallel structure.

5.B.6
Nonparallel
Constructions

Words:	*Working* and *playing* are both important.
Phrases:	Both *at home* and *at the office* she is well organized.
Clauses:	I will cut the grass *when my back is better* and *when the mower is repaired.*

Following are some examples of nonparallel constructions, along with some ways to correct them.

Nonparallel:	*To write* was easier for her than *talking.*
Parallel:	*Writing* was easier for her than *talking.*
Nonparallel:	He enjoys playing *golf, tennis,* and *to play softball.*
Parallel:	He enjoys playing *golf, tennis,* and *softball.*
Nonparallel:	*Having checked our bags* and *since we had said good-by,* we boarded the plane.
Parallel:	Since we *had checked our bags* and *had said good-by,* we boarded the plane.
Nonparallel:	The homeowners association *maintains the entrances* and *is conducting a mosquito abatement program.*
Parallel:	The homeowners association *maintains the entrances* and *conducts a mosquito abatement program.*

Whenever you use modifying words, phrases, and clauses, be sure that the relationship between the modifier and the word it modifies is clear. Avoid the common problems of dangling, squinting, and misplaced modifiers.

5.B.7
Problems with
Modifiers

Dangling modifiers are adjective phrases and clauses that are not connected to any word or phrase in the sentence. These danglers cause confusion; the reader does not know what they modify. Following are examples of dangling modifiers, along with some ways to correct them.

5.B.7.a
Dangling
Modifiers

Dangling: *Hanging the curtains,* the rod slipped and hit him on the head.
Correct: When *he was hanging the curtains,* the rod slipped and hit him on the head.

Dangling: *Young and alone,* the city can be a frightening place.
Correct: *Young and alone, she* was frightened by the city.
Young and alone, a person can be frightened by the city.

Dangling: *To complete the project on time,* the typewriter must be repaired.
Correct: *To complete the project on time, I* must have the typewriter repaired.
If the project is to be completed on time, the typewriter must be repaired.

5.B.7.b Squinting Modifiers

A *squinting modifier* is an adverb that is placed between two verbs—both of which it could modify.

The hammer that he was waving *menacingly* fell to the floor.

Look at *menacingly* once, and it seems to refer to *was waving.* Look at it again, and it seems to refer to *fell.* In other words, the modifier, *menacingly,* squints at both verbs. The writer probably meant:

The hammer that he was *menacingly* waving fell to the floor.

5.B.7.c Misplaced Modifiers

Misplaced modifiers are phrases or clauses that are not placed close enough to the word they modify. Thus they may appear to modify some word other than the one they are intended to modify. Of the three incorrect modifier constructions, the misplaced modifier is the easiest one to correct. In the following groups of sentences, the first sentence in each group has a misplaced modifier; the second has the modifier in the correct place.

Misplaced: Mary admitted to her mother *with a sad face* that she had failed the chemistry examination.
(seems to modify *mother*)
Clear: *With a sad face,* Mary admitted to her mother that she had failed the chemistry examination.

Misplaced: He keeps the awards he won *at school in his bedroom.*
Clear: *In his bedroom,* he keeps the awards he won *at school.*
The awards he won *at school* are kept *in his bedroom.*

English grammar and usage rules provide guidelines for clear communication. Every language must have rules, or people would not be able to understand one another. However, certain situations may call for some rules being "bent," or temporarily suspended. Instead of asking if a particular usage is right or wrong, it is better to ask: When is a particular usage or rule appropriate? When is it inappropriate?

5.C
Bending the Rules

In any given period, different ways of expressing the same thought may be considered correct. Today, for instance, neither of the following two sentences would raise many eyebrows.

5.C.1
Formal Versus Informal Language

"Is that the man about whom you were talking?"
"Is that the man you were talking about?"

The first sentence is formal; the second, informal. The first sentence follows all strict grammatical rules. The second breaks the rule against ending sentences with prepositions.

Different audiences have different expectations and call for different degrees of formality.

An English teacher, for instance, may expect—and even require—that you follow every grammar rule to the letter. You may give a speech on graduation night or submit an application to a college or technical school or enter a report on a scientific experiment for first-prize consideration at a local science fair.

In the previous examples, the people reading or hearing what you have to say will probably expect you to follow grammar and usage rules strictly to indicate your overall knowledge. This does not mean, however, that they expect you to be stuffy or boring. It is entirely possible to follow the rules and still communicate vividly.

However, formal expression is not always appropriate. Highly formal language used in a highly informal situation may give your readers or listeners the impression that you feel superior to them. Sometimes, writing that is close to normal speech patterns communicates best. In those cases, you might choose to bend some of the rules of formal grammar and usage. *See* **5.C.4**: Commonly Bent Rules.

5.C.2
Considering
Your Audience

Even when you bend the rules, it is important to consider your readers' and listeners' expectations. For instance, there may be a great difference between the language in a letter you write to your great-aunt Harriet and that in a letter you send to your friend Judi. These letters are both examples of informal writing, but they will differ because of your knowledge of the intended reader. Your great-aunt Harriet may not care to read slang expressions that she may or may not understand. Judi, on the other hand, might feel you were being stiff and unfriendly if you did not express yourself as you do when you are talking to her in person. You may bend the formal rules in both letters, but you may bend them in different ways.

Dear Aunt Harriet,

Thank you so much for my beautiful birthday present. It's my first cashmere sweater! I love it, and it matches both my tan skirt and my plaid skirt. Three people have already asked to borrow it.

Love,
Zelda

Dear Judi,

You'll never guess what my aunt sent me. A cashmere sweater! Couldn't you just die! I wish I could wear it every day, it's so cool. Annie Biggs turned green.

Write soon,
Zelda

Aside from the rule bending that occurs naturally in informal communication, rule bending is also a device used intentionally in various kinds of writing such as fiction, poetry, and advertising. For instance, writers who wish to create their own individual styles sometimes ignore certain rules completely.

5.C.3 Rule Bending in Creative Writing and Advertising

Newspaper columnist Don Marquis claimed that his column was written by a cockroach who could not operate the shift key on the typewriter. Thus, his entire work, compiled as *archy and mehitabel,* was written with no capital letters.

The poet e.e. cummings disregarded many rules of grammar and punctuation in his search for a fresh and spontaneous approach. He made up words, ran words and sentences together, and rarely used capital letters. (That is why he always spelled his name e.e. cummings.)

5.C.4
Commonly
Bent Rules

Rule bendings are common tools of authors seeking to be original or to attract attention. Writers have a problem that speakers do not: they cannot whisper or shout. They cannot gesture or use body movement to catch their readers' attention. Writers must use the tools of writing to make the reader sit up and take notice. Sometimes, the best way to attract the reader is to present material in a strikingly different way.

Advertising is an example of a kind of writing where little attention is paid to rules. For example, standard rules of capitalization are often abandoned, and whole sentences may appear in capital letters. This is one way that a writer can shout.

FREE!
PRIZES! TRAVEL! MONEY!
ONE DAY ONLY!

Some advertising is designed to whisper. But since writers want the whisper to get our attention, they bend some rules.

preferred customers only . . .
conroy studio invites . . .
the selby gallery announces . . .

Advertising writers also frequently make use of sentence fragments, those nonsentences that students are warned to avoid. When every word counts (and costs) in an advertisement, the writer may "economize" by including only the essentials.

A real opportunity!
Unbelievable savings!
The chance of a lifetime!

Even if you are not an advertising writer, a dramatist, a novelist, or a poet, you will frequently bend the rules in response to the audience, the situation, and the tone you wish to communicate. Following are examples and explanations of eight of the most commonly bent rules.

Do not end a sentence with a preposition.
This rule is often quoted but, except in examinations and highly formal usage, it is rarely followed. Some sentences sound fine when they are composed to follow the rules.

> Mr. Johnson is the county official to whom we sent our complaint.
>
> To what do you owe your great success?

Other sentences, however, sound unnecessarily stiff and unnatural when they follow the rule.

> Of what could the coach be thinking?
> That is the fence over which we climbed.

Your best guideline for breaking this rule is to listen to how the sentence sounds. Unless a teacher insists that you never end a sentence with a preposition, use your judgment and opt for the version of the sentence that seems most natural. Remember Winston Churchill's complaint against rigidly following the rule forbidding end prepositions. "That," he snorted, "is the kind of nonsense up with which I will not put!"

Do not split infinitives.
A split infinitive occurs when an adverb comes between "to" and the stem of a verb.

> Jack and Walter decided *to* simply *stay* home.
> The recipe says *to* thoroughly *mix* the batter.

In the past, there was a hard-and-fast rule against splitting infinitives, and some teachers still insist on this rule. Most sentences can be written to avoid split infinitives. For example, the preceding two sentences can be written as follows:

> Jack and Walter decided simply *to stay* home.
> The recipe says *to mix* the batter thoroughly.

However, it is now increasingly common to avoid split infinitives only when they create an awkward sentence, as in the following example.

> **Awkward:**   She wanted *to* quickly *paint* the kitchen.
> **Better:**   She wanted *to paint* the kitchen quickly.

In most other situations, it is now considered acceptable to split infinitives.

> Jack seems *to* gladly *take* on projects nobody else wants to handle.

In some cases, it may actually be preferable to split infinitives rather than to create awkward or unclear sentences.

Awkward: I was unable fully *to appreciate* the program.
Better: I was unable *to* fully *appreciate* the program.

Unclear: *To chew* gum constantly ruins your image.
(does *constantly* modify *chew* or *ruin*?)
Better: *To* constantly *chew* gum ruins your image.

5.C.4.c
Who Versus
Whom

Use who *in the nominative case, but* whom *in the objective case.*

While this rule is still followed in formal speech and writing, the use of the relative pronoun *whom* is growing less and less common when the word appears at the beginning of a sentence or a clause.

Formal: *Whom* will you invite to the party?
Informal: *Who* will you invite to the party?

Formal: That is the man *whom* my father wanted to meet.
Informal: That is the man *who* my father wanted to meet.

Whom is still frequently used even in informal speech when it directly follows a preposition.

Is that the girl *to whom* you wrote a note?
Mr. Johnson is the grocer *for whom* I work.

Note, however, that such sentences can avoid the *who/whom* questions by a slight rewrite that bends the rule against ending sentences with prepositions. Then the relative pronoun can be dropped entirely.

Is that the girl you wrote the note to?
Mr. Davis is the grocer I work for.

5.C.4.d
I Versus Me

Use "It's I" not "It's me."

Formal rules hold that the predicate nominative always takes the nominative case and that "It's I" is therefore the only correct construction.

Most grammarians, however, believe that it is perfectly acceptable to say "It's me." The more formal construction is still advisable when the subject and the verb are not contracted: "It is I."

NOTE: It is not considered proper to use the objective case for third-person pronouns.

Incorrect:	It's him	It's her	It's them
Correct:	It's he	It's she	It's they

In the future tense, use shall *for the first person and* will *for the second and third person conjugations. To show special determination, use* will *for the first person and* shall *for the second and third person.*

According to formal grammar rules, "I *shall* go" means "I plan to go," and "I *will* go" means "I am determined to go and nothing will change my plans." Likewise, "you *will* go," "he or she *will* go," and "they *will* go" indicate intention to go, while "you *shall* go," "he or she *shall* go," and "they *shall* go" indicate special determination.

In informal use, all these distinctions have been fading. First, second, and third person all use the auxiliary *will* in the future tense, and special determination is seldom indicated. When it is, *shall* is used to indicate determination for all three persons.

5.C.4.e
Shall* Versus *Will

Use the subjunctive for statements that are doubtful, conditional, unreal, or improbable.

In formal usage, the subjunctive is still used for such statements.

> If I *were* five years younger, I would sign up for that roller-skating class.

> If Sally *were* able to sew, she would help make the costumes for the play.

In informal usage, the indicative mood is frequently used in place of the subjunctive.

> If I *was* five years younger, I would sign up for that roller-skating class.

> If Sally *was* able to sew, she would help you with the costumes for the play.

5.C.4.f
Subjunctive Mood

Do not begin sentences with conjunctions.

Formal grammar rules state that sentences should not start with coordinating conjunctions. However, many sentences can communicate extra force and interest when this rule is bent, as in the following examples.

> Sandra thought she knew everything there was to know about her friend Jackie. *But* she was wrong.

> Ralph predicted that everyone would show up just when the hardest jobs were already finished. *And* that's exactly what happened.

5.C.4.g
Conjunctions Starting Sentences

**5.C.4.h.
Sentence
Fragments**

Do not use sentence fragments.

A *sentence fragment* is a group of words that does not contain both a subject and a predicate. Although it is generally wise to follow the rule forbidding sentence fragments, fragments can sometimes be used effectively for special impact.

> Johnny thinks Marsha doesn't like him. *Not so!*

> Will the Allentown Alligators beat the Bordentown Bears tonight? *Hard to say.*

Clichés to Avoid

Clichés are expressions that have lost their impact through overuse. Many similes are clichés.

> eyes like stars   hungry as a bear

Clichés are also found in business letters and reports and academic papers.

> enclosed you will find   this will inform you

The following list includes many common clichés and some possible replacement phrases. Words and phrases marked with an asterisk (*) are superfluous. They should be avoided whenever possible. These clichés are especially likely to be overused in business communications. If you can eliminate them, you will get your meaning across more successfully. Watch for worn-out phrases in your writing so you can fix them—but don't substitute other clichés!

Clichés to Avoid

CLICHÉ	REPLACEMENT
abreast of the times	current
according to Hoyle	by the rules
according to the record	the record shows that
aching void	emptiness
acid test	conclusive test
acknowledge defeat	admit defeat
after all is said and done	really
ahead of schedule	early
all in all	altogether
almost never	seldom
along the same lines	similarly
and like that	in that way
answering yours of	*

CLICHÉ	REPLACEMENT
anticipating your order/reply	*
are of the opinion	think; believe
as luck would have it	fortunately; unfortunately
as per	*
as regards	*
at a loss for words	speechless
at the present time	today; now
bathed in tears	sobbing
beg to advise/assure	*
best bet	best decision
bitter end	end
bolt from the blue	surprise
bottom line	total; goal
budding genius	genius
busy as a bee	extremely busy
by and large	generally
by force of circumstances	because
by leaps and bounds	fast
by the skin of one's teeth	barely
captain of the ship	head
center of attention	focus
check to cover	*
checkered career	bad record
clinging vine	dependent person
colossal mistake	bad error
come into conflict	conflict (verb)
compare favorably	compare well
conduct an investigation	investigate
conspicuous by one's absence	missed
contact	call, consult, telephone, see, write
cook one's goose	harm; ruin
cooperate together	cooperate
cost the sum of	cost
create the possibility	enable
deadly earnest	serious
doom to failure	ensure failure
down in the dumps	miserable
due in large measure to	due largely to
duly noted	*
each and every	all
enclosed please find	*
endeavor	try
epic struggle	prolonged fight
equal to the occasion	able
every fiber of one's being	completely
fabricate	lie
fair sex	women

CLICHÉ	REPLACEMENT
familiar landmark	landmark
few and far between	rare
first and foremost	first
fit as a fiddle	fit
fly off the handle	rage
footprints in the sands of time	past events
for a period of a week	for a week
for all intents and purposes	seemingly
for the purpose of	in order to; to
for your files	*
for your information	*
free as the breeze	free; carefree
get down to brass tacks	get serious
give encouragement to	encourage
give rise to	cause
go without saying	be obvious
goodly number	many
green as grass	green
green with envy	envious
have need for	need
heartfelt gratitude	thanks
heart's content	satisfaction
heated argument	serious argument
hereby advise	*
hold promise	look promising
holy state of matrimony	marriage
hoping your order	*
I am, we are [ending last sentence]	*
I have your letter of	*
in a most careful manner	meticulously
in all cases	always
in due course	*
in hot water	in trouble
in one fell swoop	in one step
in receipt of	*
in reference to	*
in terms of	regarding
in the amount of	for
in the bag	certain
in the depths of despair	depressed
in the event that	if
in the final analysis	finally
in the near future	soon
in the neighborhood of	about
in this day and age	today, now
inaugurate	begin
indigenous	native
initial	first

CLICHÉ	REPLACEMENT
iron will	determination
irony of fate	irony
it goes without saying	obviously
it should be understood	understand that
it stands to reason	logically
it's a cinch	definitely
kind order	*
kindly advise	*
knock the tar out of	beat
large number of	many
last but not least	last
last straw	end
like a bull in a china shop	clumsy; clumsily
like an old shoe	worn out; comfortable
look for all the world like	look like
majority of	most of
make inquiries regarding	ask
mantle of snow	layer of snow
maximum	most
may we suggest	*
method in one's madness	method
minimum	least
month of Sundays	long time
need no introduction	be well-known
nip in the bud	stop
no one of right mind	no one
none the worse for wear	in good condition
of a confidential nature	confidential
of the above date	*
optimum	best
paramount issue	critical issue
permit us to remind	*
picturesque scene	lovely scene
please accept/find/note/rest assured	*
pleasing prospect	good idea
powers that be	authorities
promising future	likely success
put one's nose to the grindstone	work hard
put words in one's mouth	influence
race, color, or creed	origin, beliefs
rant and rave	rant
recent date	*
referring to yours of	*
regarding the matter	*
regret to advise/inform/state	*
reign supreme	rule
right and proper	correct

CLICHÉ	REPLACEMENT
sadder but wiser	experienced
safe to say	reasonable
sea of faces	crowd
self-made person	entrepreneur
significantly reduce	greatly reduce
skeleton in the closet	secret
skin alive	punish
spill the beans	blurt
strong as an ox	powerful
stubborn as a mule	obstinate
sturdy as an oak	strong
substantial portion	many, much
take into consideration	think about
take into custody	arrest
take one's word for	believe
take pleasure in	enjoy
take the easy way out	find an easy solution
take the liberty of	*
than meets the eye	than is obvious
thanking you in advance	thank you for
thereby hangs the tale	that's the reason
time marches on	time passes
time of one's life	best time
too funny for words	hilarious
trusting to have	*
under separate cover	mailed separately
upset the applecart	disturb
utilize	use
valued favor/order	*
venture a suggestion	suggest
walk of life	career
way of life	beliefs
we are pleased to advise/note	*
weaker sex	women
where angels fear to tread	where there's danger
widespread use	regular use; regularly
wish to advise/state	*
with bated breath	nervously
with reference to	about
without further delay	immediately
words fail to express	I can't describe
wreak havoc	bring disaster
your kind indulgence	*
your letter of recent date	*
your Mr./Ms. _____	Mr./Ms. _____
your valued patronage	*

The following list includes forms of address for some officials and dignitaries whom you may have occasion to address in speaking or writing. Not all possible dignitary titles are included, nor are the forms of address given necessarily the only correct ones.

The forms given under "In speaking" are the titles that should be used when you speak in person to these officials. The forms listed under "Writing the address," "Salutation," and "Closing" should be used when you write business letters to officials. *See* **9.A**: Personal Letter Format *and* **12.B.1**: Business Letter Format. *See also* **18.C**: Speaking to Specialists and Professionals. Address forms are the same for women as for men, except where indicated.

5.E

Proper Forms of Address

President of the United States.

In speaking:	Mr. President *or* Sir Madam President *or* Madam
Writing the address:	The President The White House Washington, DC 20500
Salutation:	Dear Mr. *or* Madam President:
Closing:	Respectfully,

**5.E.1
United States
Officials**

Vice President of the United States.

In speaking:	Mr. Vice President *or* Sir Madam Vice President *or* Madam
Writing the address:	The Vice President United States Senate Washington, DC 20510
Salutation:	Dear Mr. *or* Madam Vice President:
Closing:	Respectfully,

Cabinet Members (Except Attorney General).

In speaking:	Mr. Secretary *or* Mr. Green Madam Secretary *or* Miss, Mrs., *or* Ms. Smith
Writing the address:	The Honorable John Green Secretary of State
Salutation:	Dear Mr. *or* Madam Secretary: *or* Dear Secretary Green:
Closing:	Sincerely yours,

Attorney General.

In speaking:	Mr. *or* Madam Attorney General
Writing the address:	The Attorney General
Salutation:	Dear Mr. *or* Madam Attorney General:
Closing:	Sincerely yours,

Chief Justice of the United States.

In speaking:	Mr. *or* Madam Chief Justice
Writing the address:	The Chief Justice of the United States Supreme Court Building Washington, DC 20543
Salutation:	Dear Mr. *or* Madam Chief Justice:
Closing:	Sincerely yours,

Associate Justices of the Supreme Court.

In speaking:	Mr. *or* Madam Justice *or* Mr. *or* Madam Justice Green
Writing the address:	Mr. *or* Madam Justice Green
Salutation:	Dear Mr. *or* Madam Justice: *or* Dear Mr. *or* Madam Justice Green:
Closing:	Sincerely yours,

United States Senators.

In speaking:	Senator Green
Writing the address:	The Honorable Mary Green United States Senate Washington, DC 20510
Salutation:	Dear Senator: *or* Dear Senator Green:
Closing:	Sincerely yours,

United States Representatives.

In speaking:	Mr. *or* Miss, Mrs., *or* Ms. Smith
Writing the address:	The Honorable Mary Smith House of Representatives Washington, DC 20515

Salutation:	Dear Mr. *or* Ms. Smith: *or* Dear Representative Smith: *or* Dear Congressman *or* Congresswoman Smith:
Closing:	Sincerely yours,

United States Ambassadors.

In speaking:	Mr. *or* Madam Ambassador
Writing the address:	The Honorable John Green Ambassador of the United States of America
Salutation:	Sir: *or* Madam: *or* Dear Mr. *or* Madam Ambassador:
Closing:	Very truly yours, *or* Sincerely yours,

> **NOTE:** Although it is permissible to refer to a United States ambassador as an "American ambassador," it is best not to do so, because other western hemisphere ambassadors are also conscious of being Americans.

Governors.

In speaking:	Governor Smith
Writing the address:	The Honorable Mary Smith Governor of Tennessee
Salutation:	Sir: *or* Madam: *or* Dear Governor Smith:
Closing:	Respectfully, *or* Sincerely yours,

State Senators and Representatives.

State legislators are addressed in the same manner as United States senators and representatives.

Mayors.

In speaking:	Mayor Green *or* Mr. *or* Madam Mayor
Writing the address:	The Honorable John Green
Salutation:	Sir: *or* Madam: *or* Dear Mayor Green:
Closing:	Sincerely yours,

157

Judges.

In speaking: Mr. *or* Madam Justice
Writing the address: The Honorable Mary Smith
Salutation: Sir: *or* Madam:
Closing: Sincerely yours,

5.E.2 Canadian Officials

Governor General.

In speaking: Your Excellency
Writing the address: His *or* Her Excellency
The Right Honourable John
     Green
Governor General of Canada
Government House
Ottawa, Ontario K1A OA1
Salutation: Sir: *or* Madam:
or Dear Sir:
or Dear Madam:
Closing: Respectfully,

Prime Minister.

In speaking: Your Excellency
or Mr. *or* Madam Prime
     Minister
Writing the address: The Right Honourable Mary
     Smith, P.C., M.P.
Prime Minister of Canada
Ottawa, Ontario K1A 0A2
Salutation: Sir: *or* Madam:
or Dear Sir: *or* Dear Madam:
Closing: Very truly yours,
or Sincerely yours,

Senators.

In speaking: Sir *or* Madam *or* Senator Green
Writing the address: The Honourable John Green
The Senate
Ottawa, Ontario KA1 OA4
Salutation: Dear Sir *or* Madam:
Closing: Yours sincerely,

Members of the House of Commons.

In speaking:	Sir *or* Madam *or* Mr. *or* Ms. Green
Writing the address:	Mary Green, M.P. House of Commons Ottawa, Ontario, K1A 0A6
Salutation:	Dear Sir *or* Madam:
Closing:	Yours sincerely,

Ambassadors to the United States.

In speaking:	Mr. *or* Madam Ambassador
Writing the address:	His *or* Her Excellency The Ambassador of Australia
Salutation:	Sir: *or* Madam: *or* Dear Mr. *or* Dear Madam Ambassador:
Closing:	Yours very truly,

5.E.3
Foreign Officials in the United States

Secretary-General of the United Nations.

In speaking:	Mr. *or* Madam Secretary- General
Writing the address:	His *or* Her Excellency John Green Secretary-General of the United Nations
Salutation:	Sir: *or* Madam: *or* Dear Mr. *or* Madam Secretary-General:
Closing:	Yours very truly,

(For ambassadors and representatives to the United Nations, use the form "Representative of Brazil to the United Nations.")

The correct form for closing most business letters to the clergy is "Respectfully yours" and for closing social letters, "Sincerely yours."

5.E.4
Members of the Clergy

Bishops.

In speaking:	Bishop Green
Writing the address:	The Reverend John Green Bishop of Chicago
Salutation:	Dear Bishop Green:

("The Very Reverend" is often used for Episcopal and Greek Orthodox bishops. "The Most Reverend" is often used for Roman Catholic Bishops.)

Cardinals.

In speaking:	Your Eminence
Writing the address:	His Eminence John Cardinal Green Archbishop of Chicago
Salutation:	Dear Cardinal Green:
Closing:	I have the honor to be, Your Eminence, Respectfully yours,

Ministers.

In speaking:	Reverend Green *or* Doctor Green
Writing the address:	The Reverend John Green The Reverend Mary Smith
Salutation:	Dear Reverend Green: *or* Dear Dr. Green:

Rabbis.

In speaking:	Rabbi Green *or* Doctor Green
Writing the address:	Rabbi John Green
Salutation:	Dear Rabbi Green:

Priests.

In speaking:	Father Green
Writing the address:	The Reverend John Green
Salutation:	Dear Father Green:

President or Chancellor of a University.

In speaking:	President Green *or* Chancellor Smith
Writing the address:	President John Green Chancellor Mary Smith
Salutation:	Dear President Green: Dear Chancellor Smith:
Closing:	Very truly yours, *or* Sincerely yours,

Professors.

In speaking:	Professor Smith *or* Doctor Smith
Writing the address:	Professor Mary Smith Department of Music University of Oklahoma
Salutation:	Dear Professor Smith:
Closing:	Very truly yours, *or* Sincerely yours,

**5.E.5
Academics**

Chapter

6 Mechanics

The *mechanics* of writing include rules for capitalization and punctuation. Mastering them can impart clarity to your writing.

6.A

Capitalization

Capital letters act as signals to readers. They distinguish proper nouns and adjectives from common nouns and adjectives. They announce new sentences and the beginning of direct quotations. *See also* **Chapter 4**: Grammar *and* **Chapter 5**: Usage and Style.

Knowing when to use capital letters and when to use lower-case letters can sometimes be confusing. The following list includes some general rules to observe for capitalization.

Capitalize:

1. proper nouns.

    James Smith   San Francisco   Declaration of Independence
    Arbor Day   Lake Michigan   Big Dipper

2. proper adjectives. *Proper adjectives* are adjectives that are formed from proper nouns, and proper nouns that are used as adjectives.

    American tourist   Shakespearean drama   Chinese art
    Iowa farmers   New England states   Texas chili

    Do *not* capitalize the following words. Even though they are derived from proper nouns, their use is now considered common enough that they are no longer capitalized.

anglicize	frankfurter (hot dog)	platonic friendship
bohemian life-style	japan (varnish)	quixotic
chinaware	macadam road	turkish towel
derby hat	pasteurized milk	vulcanize

3. the pronoun *I* and the interjection *O.*

Rejoice, O ye people, for I bring you glad tidings.

4. words that show family relationships when they are used instead of a name or as part of a name.

I asked Mother if Uncle John was coming.

Do *not* capitalize these words when they are preceded by a possessive, such as *my, your, their.*

My mother and uncle visited your grandfather.

5. nicknames and other identifying names.

Babe Ruth   the Sun King   Richard the Lion-Hearted

6. special titles when they immediately precede a person's name. *See also* **5.E**: Proper Forms of Address.

General Patton   Governor Ella Grasso   Pope John Paul II

Do *not* capitalize them when they follow the name.

Ella T. Grasso, governor of Connecticut
George S. Patton was a great American general.

7. professional titles and their abbreviations when they follow a personal name.

Jan Smith, M.D.   Jane Doe, Doctor of Philosophy
Maria Ames, R.N.   Leslie Jones, Doctor of Law

8. personified nouns.

She was called by Destiny to clear a path for Justice.

9. brand names.

Comet (cleanser)   Cougar (car)   Rice Krispies (cereal)

10. specific political and geographical locations (and the adjectives derived from them).

Chicago   Cook County   Asia   Asian

11. the names of all nationalities, races, and tribes (and the adjectives derived from them).

German   Japanese   Sioux   Nordic   Caucasian

12. words of direction when they are used to designate a specific place.

North Pole   Far East   Middle West   the South

Do *not* capitalize *north, south, east,* and *west* when they refer to a direction or a section of a state.

We live west of Chicago and vacation in northern Michigan.

13. the names of specific geographic features and the common nouns that are part of the proper names.

Mississippi River   Rocky Mountains   Pacific Ocean

But:

the Mississippi and Ohio rivers   the falls of the Niagara

14. the names of buildings, monuments, streets, bridges, parks, and other specific locations, and the common nouns that are part of the proper names.

White House   Grant Park   Statue of Liberty
Brooklyn Bridge   Fifth Avenue   U.S. Route 34

15. the names of organizations, business firms, and institutions.

League of Women Voters   General Foods Corporation
Northwestern University   Burnsville High School

16. the names of political parties and religious denominations and their members.

Republican Party   Roman Catholic   Islam
Democrat   Presbyterian   Buddhism

17. the names of sacred writings and of specific creeds, confessions of faith, and prayers.

Bible   Talmud   Koran
Apostles' Creed   Hail Mary   Lord's Prayer

18. nouns and pronouns that refer to a specific deity.

God   Allah   Jehovah   Zeus   Queen of Heaven
Trust in Him for He is good.

But:

The Romans believed in many gods.

19. specific cultural and historical events, wars, treaties, laws, and documents.

Reign of Terror   World War II   Treaty of Vers
Homestead Act   Articles of Confederation

20. the names of historical and cultural periods.

Renaissance   Roaring Twenties   Era of Good Feeling

But:

colonial period   Elizabethan era

21. the names of specific branches, departments, and other divisions of government.

House of Commons   Department of State   Supreme Court
Chicago Park District   Library of Congress

But:

traffic court   the city council

22. the names of specific awards and prizes.

Nobel Peace Prize   Academy Award   Medal of Honor

23. the names of specific trains, planes, ships, satellites, and submarines. (These specific names are also italicized or underlined.)

Orient Express   *Spirit of St. Louis*
Lusitania   *Skylab*   *Nautilus*

24. the names of stars, planets, constellations, and other astronomical designations.

Big Dipper   Milky Way   North Star
Mars   Ursa Major   Earth

But:

the earth   the sun   the moon

25. the days of the week, months of the year, and holidays. Lower-case the seasons of the year.

Tuesday   October   Memorial Day   Fourth of July
spring   summer   fall   winter

26. the first word of a sentence or a word or phrase that has the force of a sentence.

The children are running across the street.
Stop!   Wow!

27. the first word of a direct quotation.

"We're leaving tomorrow," said Mary.
Jane replied, "Have a good trip."

Do *not* capitalize the first quoted word after a speaker tag that interrupts a quoted sentence.

"I wish," Pete said longingly, "the whole family could go together."

28. the first word of a complete statement following a colon (:).

Here is my decision: You will not be promoted.

29. the first word (and proper names) in the salutation and the first word of the complimentary close of a letter. *See also* **9.A**: Personal Letter Format *and* **12.B.1**: Business Letter Format.

Dear Ms. Kline: Yours truly,
My dear Ellen: Sincerely yours,
                         With love,

30. the first word and all important words in the titles of works of art, books, magazines, newspapers, poems, songs, articles, television shows, plays, reports, and other writing.

The Thinker   *The Last Supper*
The Saturday Evening Post *Sun-Times*
The Skin of Our Teeth   "Murphy Brown"
A Christmas Carol   "The Raven"

31. the parts of a book when reference is made from one part to another of the same book.

The sources for this information are listed in the Bibliography.

But:

A bibliography is a list of sources.

6.B
Punctuation

Punctuation has one purpose: to make writing clear. Punctuation marks substitute for the natural pauses or changes in inflection you would use if speaking the written material. *See* **14.A.2**: Vocal Characteristics.

6.B.1
Periods

A *period* (.) is used:

1. at the end of complete declarative sentences and of commands given without emphasis. *See* **4.C**: Kinds of Sentences.

The sun was shining.   Please, wash the car.

2. after each number or letter that begins a heading in an outline. *See also* **10.A.5**: Outlining.

Why I Like Sports
I. A way to improve my health
    A. By exercising indoors
        1. Weight training

3. after initials, abbreviations, and after each part of some abbreviations.

E.W. Smith, Inc.   Dr.   ft.   Ms.   U.S.   C.O.D.

The abbreviations for some organizations and government agencies do *not* use periods. *See also* **6.C**: Postal Abbreviations of States.

FBI   VISTA   ABC   IBM

6.B.2 Question Marks

A *question mark* (?) is used:

1. at the end of direct questions. *See* **4.C**: Kinds of Sentences.

Why did you buy that car?

2. at the end of statements ending with a question.

That was silly, wasn't it?

3. after words or sentences that indicate a question.

You're leaving now?
Why?

6.B.3 Exclamation Points

An *exclamation point* (!) is used:

1. after a word, phrase, or sentence expressing strong feeling. *See* **4.C**: Kinds of Sentences.

Yuch! That tastes awful.   What a beautiful day!

2. to emphasize a command or a strong point of view.

Go away!
Okay, I'll forget about it!

3. to show amusement, sarcasm, or irony.

I'm supposed to fix supper while you read the paper!

6.B.4
Colons

A *colon* (:) is used:

1. after a complete sentence followed by a list.

Executives carry many things in their briefcases: reports, newspapers, and brown-bag lunches.

2. after a statement followed by a clause that further explains the statement.

Working women often find themselves with a double work-load: They have an income-producing job and the housework.

3. after the salutation of a business letter. *See also* **12.B.1**: Business Letter Format.

Dear Sir or Madam: Dear Ms. Williams:

4. to separate hours from minutes.

6:30 a.m.

5. to separate parts of a citation.

Genesis 1:15

6. to separate a book's title and subtitle.

Germany: A Modern History

7. to set off the speaker from the spoken words in a script.

CHARLES: What is going on here?

6.B.5
Commas

A *comma* (,) is used:

1. to separate long coordinate clauses of a compound sentence.

She could go to college now, but she would rather wait a year.

2. between words, phrases, or clauses in a series.

Jane carried her coat, hat, and gloves.
I washed the dishes, Joe dried them, and Sam put them away.

3. to set off phrases and dependent clauses that precede the main clause of a sentence. *See also* **4.B**: Parts of a Sentence.

By taking the tollway, we saved fifteen minutes.
Although the children were tired, they continued playing.

4. to set off phrases, clauses, or appositives that are not essential to the meaning of the sentence. *See also* **4.B.3**: Phrases *and* **4.B.4**: Clauses.

The nurses, kind as they were, couldn't replace Mother.
Mr. Garcia, the office manager, is well-organized.

5. to set off coordinate phrases modifying the same noun.

Her hair is as long as, but darker than, mine is.

6. between parts of a sentence suggesting contrast or comparison.

The more time you take now, the less you'll have later.

7. to indicate the omission of one or more words.

The eggs were runny; the bacon, greasy; and the toast, burnt.

8. to separate identical or similar words in a sentence.

Walk in, in groups of three.

9. to separate words that might be mistakenly joined when reading a sentence.

Soon after, the bridge was closed for repairs.

10. to set off words that introduce a sentence (*first, second, yes, no, oh*); and to set off words that suggest a break in thought (*however, namely, of course*).

No, I can't do that.   First, write down your name.
The car broke down, of course, before I got to work.

11. to set off the name of a person spoken to.

Kevin, your bicycle is across the street.
Your bicycle, Kevin, is across the street.

12. to set off a short quotation from the speaker tag.

"I'll order the drapes today," Mother said.
"I wish," John mused, "that this lecture would end."

13. after the salutation of a personal letter and after the complimentary close of any letter. *See also* **9.A**: Personal Letter Format *and* **12.B.1**: Business Letter Format.

Dear Mom and Dad,   With love,   Sincerely yours,

14. before any title or its abbreviation that follows a person's name.

J. E. Lopez, M.D.   Janet Brown, Dean of Students

15. to separate the parts of a date, an address, or a geographic location.

May 31, 1969   Christmas Day, 1976
We once lived at 5615 Martin Drive, Milwaukee, Wisconsin.
Disneyland is in Anaheim, California.

16. to set off groups of digits in large numbers.

6,780   42,536   103,789,450

17. to separate unrelated numbers in a sentence.

In 1979, 37,000 doctoral degrees were granted.

6.B.6
Semicolons

A *semicolon* (;) is used:

1. between parts of a compound sentence when they are not joined by the conjunctions *and, but, for, nor,* or *or. See also* **4.C**: Kinds of Sentences.

I want to finish the report now; I'll go to lunch later.

2. to separate independent clauses when the clauses are long or when the clauses already contain commas. *See also* **4.B.4**: Clauses.

Because the visibility was good, we planned to visit the observation floor of the Sears Tower; but since the elevators were not working, we toured the lobby.

3. after each clause in a series of three or more clauses. *See also* **4.B.4**: Clauses.

Lightning flashed; thunder roared; and rain poured down.

NOTE: If the clauses in the series are short, you may use either semicolons or commas. Your choice depends on how much you want to separate the clauses; semicolons create a greater pause than do commas. If the clauses are long, it is usually better to use semicolons.

4. before words like *hence, however, nevertheless, therefore,* and *thus* when they connect two independent clauses. **See** *also* **4.B.4.a**: Independent Clauses.

Today is a holiday; *therefore,* the mail will not be delivered.

5. to separate items in a list when commas are used within the items.

Attending the council meeting were Mr. Sloan, the grocer; Mrs. Bates, the banker; and Mr. Green, the florist.

6. before explanatory expressions such as *for example, for instance, that is,* and *namely* when the break in thought is greater than that suggested by a comma.

People prefer to own a home for several reasons; *namely,* the privacy of a backyard, the storage space of a basement or an attic, and the spaciousness of the rooms.

6.B.7 Dashes

A *dash* (—) is used:

1. to indicate a sudden change or break in thought.

The best way to finish that—but no, you don't want my opinion.

2. to suggest halting or hesitant speech.

"I—er—ah—can't seem to find it," she mumbled.

3. before a repeated word or expression.

He was *tired—tired* of running away from himself.

4. to emphasize or define a part of a sentence.

Marge Smith—that well-organized woman in the office—was promoted to assistant manager.

5. before a summarizing statement introduced by *all, this,* or similar words.

Fame, fortune, and position—*these* are the rewards for hard work.

NOTE: To indicate a dash, use one line (—) when writing by hand; when typing, use two hyphens (- -) for a dash. Do not leave any space between the dash and the word.

Last—but not least—is the zebra.

6.B.8
Apostrophes

An *apostrophe* (') is used:

1. to form the possessive of a noun. *See also* **4.A.1.d**: Possessives.

The Possessive Case for Nouns

Singular possessive	Plural possessive
the tree's leaves	the boys' bicycles
Mary's hat	the Johnson's car
Charles's book	Tom and Bob's mother

NOTE: The possessive case of pronouns does *not* use an apostrophe.

hers	theirs	ours	his	its	yours

2. to show omission of one or more letters in contractions or numbers.

didn't (did not)   '79 (1979)
one o'clock (one of the clock)

3. to show plurals of numbers, letters, and words discussed as words.

two 4's   some *B*'s   too many *and*'s

6.B.9
Hyphens

A *hyphen* (-) is used:

1. when spelling out compound numbers between 21 and 99.

twenty-three   sixty-one   twenty-ninth

2. when writing out fractions used as modifiers, but *not* when fractions are used as nouns.

two-thirds majority

But:

Two thirds were counted present.

3. to avoid confusion of words that are spelled alike.

re-cover the sofa, *but* recover from the loss
re-lay the carpet, *but* a relay race

4. in some words, to avoid the awkward joining of letters.

semi-invalid   anti-intellectual

But:

cooperate

5. after a prefix when the root word begins with a capital letter.

pre-Columbian   anti-American   mid-Victorian

6. after the prefixes *all-, ex-, quasi-,* and *self-* (in most cases).

all-inclusive   ex-husband   quasi-judicial   self-help

> **NOTE:** Dictionaries vary widely in their indication and inclusion of hyphenated prefixes and compounds. To maintain a consistent style when writing a paper, refer to one dictionary. Check all compound words against that source.

7. between parts of a compound adjective when it appears before the word it modifies.

up-to-date news   hard-working man   well-known person

But:

She is well known.   It is up to date.

8. between parts of some compound nouns. (See the note following number 6 above.)

father-in-law   stay-at-home   great-grandmother

9. to divide a word at the end of a line.

DIVIDING WORDS AT ENDS OF LINES

You may divide a word only between syllables—but *not* between all syllables in all words. There are some places where you should not divide a word, even if there is a syllable break. Below and on the following page are some general guidelines for deciding where you should or should not divide words at the end of lines.

Place the hyphen at the end of the line, *not* at the beginning of the next line.

Incorrect: The bill passed through Congress, but the Pres -ident vetoed it.

Correct: The bill passed through Congress, but the Pres- ident vetoed it.

DIVIDING WORDS AT ENDS OF LINES

Do *not* divide words of one syllable, numbers expressed in figures, contractions, or abbreviations.

> thought   width   give   prayer (*not* pray-er)
> 3,416,521 (*not* 3,416-521)
> shouldn't (*not* should-n't)
> UNICEF (*not* UNI-CEF)

Do *not* divide a word if either part of the hyphenation is a word by itself and the hyphenation could cause confusion.

> piety (*not* pie-ty)   tartan (*not* tar-tan)

Divide the word as it is pronounced. But do not divide one-letter syllables or unpronounced *-ed* from the rest of the word.

> amend-ment (*not* a-mendment)
> at-tached (*not* attach-ed)

Divide a word after a prefix or before a suffix. *See* **2.B**: Affixes. But do not carry over a two-letter suffix to the next line.

> trans-portation *or* transporta-tion (*not* transpor-tation)
> mostly (*not* most-ly)

Divide closed compound words between their main parts. And divide hyphenated compounds at the hyphen.

> home-coming (*not* homecom-ing)
> self-respect (*not* self-re-spect)

Divide between double consonants. But divide after double consonants if the root word ends in the double consonant. *See also* **2.A**: Roots.

> bab-ble   run-ning   mis-sion
> pull-ing   miss-ing

Be aware that there are some exceptions to some of the rules for hyphenating prefixes and compound words. Check your dictionary whenever you are unsure about hyphenating words—whether dividing a word at the end of a line, adding a prefix, or using a compound word. *See* **2.G**: Using a Dictionary.

Quotation marks (" ") are used:

1. to enclose all parts of a *direct quotation,* the exact words spoken or written by someone else.

"I think you should condense this," said the editor, "because we're running out of space."

2. to enclose quoted words or phrases within a sentence.

My father always told me to "get a good night's sleep and eat a hearty breakfast."

Enclose a quotation within a quotation in single quotation marks.

"When I asked my father for advice, he said, 'Get a good night's sleep and eat a hearty breakfast,' " Jane explained.

3. to enclose the titles of short works of music and poetry.

"The Yellow Rose of Texas"
"O Captain! My Captain!"

4. around the titles of lectures, sermons, pamphlets, chapters of a book, and magazine articles.

"The Way of the Just" in *The Self-Made Man in America* deals with social responsibility.

5. to enclose a word or phrase explained or defined by the rest of the sentence, a technical term in nontechnical writing, and slang, irony, or well-known expressions.

To "blue-pencil" an article is to edit it.
(explained phrase)
The "pagination" in this book is out of order.
(technical term)
The "joy of motherhood" is not found in doing diapers.
(irony)

6. before the beginning of each stanza of a quoted poem and after the last stanza.

7. before each paragraph of continuous quoted material and after the last paragraph. Quotation marks are not used at the end of intermediate paragraphs. Nor are they used with indented, single-spaced quotes set off from the text.

NOTE: There are special rules for quotation marks that adjoin other punctuation.

Commas and periods are placed *inside* closing quotation marks.

"I will go now," she said, "and be back in an hour."

Semicolons and colons are placed *outside* closing quotation marks.

She said, "I'll go to the store"; but then she stayed home.

"To be or not to be": this is one of Shakespeare's most famous lines.

Question marks and exclamation points are placed *inside* the closing quotation marks if they belong to the quotation.

"What book are you reading?" he asked.
"Go now!" she ordered.

If question marks and exclamation points are *not* part of the quotation, they go *outside* the quotation marks.

Did they sing "America the Beautiful"?
I was shocked when she said quietly, "I've been fired"!

6.B.11 Parentheses

Parentheses ( ) are used:

1. to enclose explanatory material in a sentence when this material has no essential connection with the rest of the sentence.

   George Washington (1732–1799) was our first President.

2. to enclose sources of information within a sentence. *See* **11.C.4**: Parenthetical Citations.

   Cain was jealous of his brother Abel and killed him (Genesis 4:5–8).

3. around numbers or letters that indicate subdivisions of a sentence.

   There are three wedding promises: (1) to love, (2) to honor, and (3) to cherish.

4. around figures that repeat a number.

   I wrote the check for twenty-one dollars and five cents ($21.05).

Brackets [ ] are used:

1. to enclose parenthetical matter within parentheses.

Shakespeare's most difficult tragedy (*Hamlet* [about 1600]) has been performed numerous times.

2. to correct a mistake in a direct quote.

"The chocolate mous[s]e was delicious," wrote the gourmet.

3. to indicate your own explanations or comments within direct quotations.

Kathy said, "When I get older [about six years old], I'm going to buy a dog."

4. to indicate stage and acting directions in plays.

MARY [seated, with face in her hands]: I am so depressed!

Ellipses (. . . *or* . . . .) are used:

1. with direct quotations to indicate that a word or words have been omitted. Use three spaced dots to indicate that words have been omitted at the beginning or within the quotation. Use a period and three spaced dots at the end of a sentence when additional sentences or words have been omitted.

The plants were healthy because Roger ". . . took care of them devotedly."

"The gardener . . . took care of them devotedly."

"The men and women who pushed the frontier westward . . . probably never thought of themselves as brave. . . . But most faced danger, nevertheless."

2. to indicate words omitted at the end of a sentence. (Use four spaced dots [the first dot is the period].)

"The gardener loved the plants and shrubs. . . ."

A *virgule* (/) is used:

1. between two words to indicate that the meaning of either word could apply.

My son and/or my daughter will be home.

6.B.12
Brackets

6.B.13
Ellipses

6.B.14
Virgules

2. as a dividing line in dates, fractions, and abbreviations.

5/29/98   5/8   c/o (in care of)

3. with a run-in passage of poetry to indicate where one line ends and another begins.

"All the world's a stage,/ And all the men and women merely players./ They have their exits and their entrances;/ And one man in his time plays many parts,/ His acts being seven ages."

6.B.15
Italics or Underlining

Italics or *underlining* (*italics* <u>underlining</u>) is used:

1. for the titles of books, plays, long poems, magazines, and newspapers.

Gone with the Wind   *Hamlet*   *Paradise Lost*
Newsweek   *The Tuscaloosa News*

2. for titles of paintings and other works of art.

The Blue Boy   *Venus de Milo*

3. for names of specific ships, planes, trains, spacecraft, and artificial satellites.

Titanic   *Spirit of St. Louis*   *Orient Express*
Voyager 2   *Sputnik*

4. for any foreign word that is not commonly used in English. These words have labels (such as *Latin, French,* or *Italian*) in the dictionary. *See* <u>2.G</u>: Using a Dictionary.

Jimmy was an *enfant terrible*.
The commencement speaker went on *ad infinitum*.

5. for any words, letters, or numbers considered as words.

A, an, and *the* are articles.
Cross your *t*'s and dot your *i*'s.
The *7*'s in multiplication were hard, but the *10*'s were easy.

NOTE: Remember that words appear in italics when set in type (as in books or magazines); they are underlined when you write by hand or use a typewriter.

When you use the name of a state in narrative writing, spell it out. But when you mention a state name in an address or a list, use the two-letter abbreviation preferred by the United States Post Office. This abbreviation does not include a period or other punctuation, just two capital letters as shown in the following list.

6.C
Postal Abbreviations of States

Postal Abbreviations

STATE	ABBREVIATION	STATE	ABBREVIATION
Alabama	AL	Montana	MT
Alaska	AK	Nebraska	NE
Arizona	AZ	Nevada	NV
Arkansas	AR	New Hampshire	NH
California	CA	New Jersey	NJ
Colorado	CO	New Mexico	NM
Connecticut	CT	New York	NY
Delaware	DE	North Carolina	NC
District of Columbia	DC	North Dakota	ND
Florida	FL	Ohio	OH
Georgia	GA	Oklahoma	OK
Hawaii	HI	Oregon	OR
Idaho	ID	Pennsylvania	PA
Illinois	IL	Puerto Rico	PR
Indiana	IN	Rhode Island	RI
Iowa	IA	South Carolina	SC
Kansas	KS	South Dakota	SD
Kentucky	KY	Tennessee	TN
Louisiana	LA	Texas	TX
Maine	ME	Utah	UT
Maryland	MD	Vermont	VT
Massachusetts	MA	Virginia	VA
Michigan	MI	Washington	WA
Minnesota	MN	West Virginia	WV
Mississippi	MS	Wisconsin	WI
Missouri	MO	Wyoming	WY

Index

A

a, an, 116
Abbreviations
  end-of-letter, 311–12
  periods after, 167
  postal, of state, 179
  virgules in, 178
ability, capability, 125
Abstract, 346–47
Abstract nouns, 64
Abstract words, 33
Academics, forms of address
  for, 161
accept, except, 125
Acronyms, 9
Action verbs, 78, 80
Active listening, 429
Active voice, 81, 208
Adam's apple, 382
adapt, adept, adopt, 125
Address, proper forms of,
  155–61
Addresses, commas in, 170
adept, adapt, adopt, 125
Adjective(s), 74. *See also*
  Modifiers
  cardinal, 74
  choice of, 77
  comparison of, 75–77
  correcting dangling
    modifiers, 141–42
  descriptive, 74
  distinguishing between
    adverb and, 97–98
  infinitive phase used as,
    106–7
  limiting, 72, 74
  numerical, 74
  ordinal, 74
  participial phase used as,
    106
  participles as, 92–93
  placement of, 75
  possessive pronouns as,
    72
  predicate, 77–78
  prepositional phrases used
    as, 105
  pronominal, 74
  proper, 162
Adjective clauses, 107–109
adjoin, adjourn, 125
Adjourn (parliamentary
  procedure), 464
adopt, adapt, adept, 125

Adverb(s), 94. *See also*
  Modifiers
  classifying by function, 95
  classifying by meaning, 95
  comparison of, 96
  conjunctive, 95
  correcting squinting
    modifiers, 142
  distinguishing between
    adjective and, 97–98
  independent, 96
  infinitive phrase used as,
    106–7
  interrogative, 95
  of manner, 96
  placement of, 98
  prepositional phrases used
    as, 105
  relative, 95
  transitional, 95
  types of, 94–95
Adverb clauses, 108
adverse, averse, 126
Advertising, rule bending in,
  145–50
advice, advise, 125
Advice, giving, in family,
  511
affect, effect, 125, 213
Affirmative side, in debate,
  453
Agenda, 464, 466–67
aggravate, irritate, 116
Agreement
  pronoun-antecedent,
    72–73, 135–36
  subject-verb, 93–94,
    133–35
agree to, agree with, 116
allay, ally, 125
all right, alright, 125
all the farther, all the faster,
  116
all together, altogether, 126
allude, elude, 126
allusion, illusion, 126
ally, allay, 125
alms, arms, 126
alright, all right, 125
also, then, 123, 132
although, though, 116
altogether, all together, 126
Amendment, 464
amiable, amicable, 126
among, between, 116
amount, number, 116

Amusement, exclamation
  point to show, 167
an, a, 116
Analogy, 34, 199, 206
Analytic approach, 267
Analyze, 269
and etc., 116
Announcements, 462
  formal, 246–47
  informal, 248
Answering machine, leaving
  message on, 433
ante, anti, 126
Antecedent, 72–73, 135–36
anti, ante, 126
anticipate, expect, 116
Antonym, 31, 38
anxious, eager, 117
anyplace, anyways, 117
anywhere, anywheres, 117
Apology, letters of, 238–40
Apostrophe
  in contractions, 172
  to show plurals of
    numbers, letters, and
    words, 172
  to show possession, 172
Appearance, in speaking, 396
Appendix, of business report,
  348
Appositives, 32, 66–67
appraise, apprise, 126
Approach, shifts in, 137
apt, liable, likely, 117
Argumentative writing,
  218–19
arms, alms, 126
Articles, 75
Articulation, 384–86, 392
Art works, italics for titles of,
  178
as, like, 121
as large as, larger than, 126
assay, essay, 126
Astronomical terms,
  capitalizing, 165
Attention-holding devices in
  speech, 413
Audience
  for newsletter, 367
  identifying, 197
  in public speaking, 407–8,
    424–26
  in writing, 144
Audio tools, 404–5